I0176469

DICTIONARY
THEME–BASED

ENGLISH-INDONESIAN

The most useful words
To expand your lexicon and sharpen
your language skills

3000 words

Theme-based dictionary British English-Indonesian - 3000 words

By Andrey Taranov

T&P Books vocabularies are intended for helping you learn, memorize and review foreign words. The dictionary is divided into themes, covering all major spheres of everyday activities, business, science, culture, etc.

The process of learning words using T&P Books' theme-based dictionaries gives you the following advantages:

- Correctly grouped source information predetermines success at subsequent stages of word memorization
- Availability of words derived from the same root allowing memorization of word units (rather than separate words)
- Small units of words facilitate the process of establishing associative links needed for consolidation of vocabulary
- Level of language knowledge can be estimated by the number of learned words

T&P Books Publishing
www.tpbooks.com

This book is also available in E-book formats.
Please visit www.tpbooks.com or the major online bookstores.

INDONESIAN THEME-BASED DICTIONARY
British English collection

T&P Books vocabularies are intended to help you learn, memorize, and review foreign words. The vocabulary contains over 3000 commonly used words arranged thematically.

- Vocabulary contains the most commonly used words
- Recommended as an addition to any language course
- Meets the needs of beginners and advanced learners of foreign languages
- Convenient for daily use, revision sessions, and self-testing activities
- Allows you to assess your vocabulary

Special features of the vocabulary

- Words are organized according to their meaning, not alphabetically
- Words are presented in three columns to facilitate the reviewing and self-testing processes
- Words in groups are divided into small blocks to facilitate the learning process
- The vocabulary offers a convenient and simple transcription of each foreign word

The vocabulary has 101 topics including:

Basic Concepts, Numbers, Colors, Months, Seasons, Units of Measurement, Clothing & Accessories, Food & Nutrition, Restaurant, Family Members, Relatives, Character, Feelings, Emotions, Diseases, City, Town, Sightseeing, Shopping, Money, House, Home, Office, Working in the Office, Import & Export, Marketing, Job Search, Sports, Education, Computer, Internet, Tools, Nature, Countries, Nationalities and more …

TABLE OF CONTENTS

PRONUNCIATION GUIDE

Letter	Indonesian example	T&P phonetic alphabet	English example
Aa	zaman	[a]	shorter than in 'ask'
Bb	besar	[b]	baby, book
Cc	kecil, cepat	[ʧ]	church, French
Dd	dugaan	[d]	day, doctor
Ee	segera, mencium	[e], [ə]	medal, elm
Ff	berfungsi	[f]	face, food
Gg	juga, lagi	[g]	game, gold
Hh	hanya, bahwa	[h]	home, have
Ii	izin, sebagai ganti	[i], [j]	Peter, yard
Jj	setuju, ijin	[dʒ']	jeans, gin
Kk	kemudian, tidak	[k], [']	kiss, glottal stop
Ll	dilarang	[l]	lace, people
Mm	melihat	[m]	magic, milk
Nn	berenang	[n], [ŋ]	name, ring
Oo	toko roti	[o:]	fall, bomb
Pp	peribahasa	[p]	pencil, private
Qq	Aquarius	[k]	clock, kiss
Rr	ratu, riang	[r]	trilled [r]
Ss	sendok, syarat	[s], [ʃ]	city, machine
Tt	tamu, adat	[t]	tourist, trip
Uu	ambulans	[u]	book
Vv	renovasi	[v]	very, river
Ww	pariwisata	[w]	vase, winter
Xx	boxer	[ks]	box, taxi
Yy	banyak, syarat	[j]	yes, New York
Zz	zamrud	[z]	zebra, please

Combinations of letters

aa	maaf	[a'a]	a+glottal stop
kh	khawatir	[h]	home, have
th	Gereja Lutheran	[t]	tourist, trip
-k	tidak	[']	glottal stop

ABBREVIATIONS
used in the dictionary

English abbreviations

ab.	-	about
adj	-	adjective
adv	-	adverb
anim.	-	animate
as adj	-	attributive noun used as adjective
e.g.	-	for example
etc.	-	et cetera
fam.	-	familiar
fem.	-	feminine
form.	-	formal
inanim.	-	inanimate
masc.	-	masculine
math	-	mathematics
mil.	-	military
n	-	noun
pl	-	plural
pron.	-	pronoun
sb	-	somebody
sing.	-	singular
sth	-	something
v aux	-	auxiliary verb
vi	-	intransitive verb
vi, vt	-	intransitive, transitive verb
vt	-	transitive verb

BASIC CONCEPTS

1. Pronouns

I, me	**saya, aku**	[saja], [aku]
you	**engkau, kamu**	[eŋkau], [kamu]
he, she, it	**beliau, dia, ia**	[beliau], [dia], [ia]
we	**kami, kita**	[kami], [kita]
you (to a group)	**kalian**	[kalian]
you (polite, sing.)	**Anda**	[anda]
you (polite, pl)	**Anda sekalian**	[anda sekalian]
they	**mereka**	[mereka]

2. Greetings. Salutations

Hello! (fam.)	**Halo!**	[halo!]
Hello! (form.)	**Halo!**	[halo!]
Good morning!	**Selamat pagi!**	[slamat pagi!]
Good afternoon!	**Selamat siang!**	[slamat siaŋ!]
Good evening!	**Selamat sore!**	[slamat sore!]
to say hello	**menyapa**	[mənjapa]
Hi! (hello)	**Hai!**	[hey!]
greeting (n)	**sambutan, salam**	[sambutan], [salam]
to greet (vt)	**menyambut**	[mənjambut]
How are you?	**Apa kabar?**	[apa kabar?]
What's new?	**Apa yang baru?**	[apa yaŋ baru?]
Goodbye!	**Selamat tinggal!**	[slamat tiŋgal!],
	Selamat jalan!	[slamat dʒʲalan!]
Bye!	**Dadah!**	[dadah!]
See you soon!	**Sampai bertemu lagi!**	[sampaj bərtemu lagi!]
Farewell! (to a friend)	**Sampai jumpa!**	[sampaj dʒʲumpa!]
Farewell! (form.)	**Selamat tinggal!**	[slamat tiŋgal!]
to say goodbye	**berpamitan**	[bərpamitan]
Cheers!	**Sampai nanti!**	[sampaj nanti!]
Thank you! Cheers!	**Terima kasih!**	[tərima kasih!]
Thank you very much!	**Terima kasih banyak!**	[tərima kasih banjaʔ!]
My pleasure!	**Kembali! Sama-sama!**	[kembali!], [sama-sama!]
Don't mention it!	**Kembali!**	[kembali!]
It was nothing	**Kembali!**	[kembali!]
Excuse me!	**Maaf, ...**	[maʔaf, ...]
to excuse (forgive)	**memaafkan**	[memaʔafkan]
to apologize (vi)	**meminta maaf**	[meminta maʔaf]
My apologies	**Maafkan saya**	[maʔafkan saja]

I'm sorry!	**Maaf!**	[ma'af!]
to forgive (vt)	**memaafkan**	[mema'afkan]
It's okay! (that's all right)	**Tidak apa-apa!**	[tida' apa-apa!]
please (adv)	**tolong**	[toloŋ]
Don't forget!	**Jangan lupa!**	[dʒ'aŋan lupa!]
Certainly!	**Tentu!**	[tentu!]
Of course not!	**Tentu tidak!**	[tentu tida'!]
Okay! (I agree)	**Baiklah! Baik!**	[bajklah!], [baj'!]
That's enough!	**Cukuplah!**	[tʃukuplah!]

3. Questions

Who?	**Siapa?**	[siapa?]
What?	**Apa?**	[apa?]
Where? (at, in)	**Di mana?**	[di mana?]
Where (to)?	**Ke mana?**	[ke mana?]
From where?	**Dari mana?**	[dari mana?]
When?	**Kapan?**	[kapan?]
Why? (What for?)	**Mengapa?**	[məŋapa?]
Why? (~ are you crying?)	**Mengapa?**	[məŋapa?]
What for?	**Untuk apa?**	[untu' apa?]
How? (in what way)	**Bagaimana?**	[bagajmana?]
What? (What kind of ...?)	**Apa? Yang mana?**	[apa?], [yaŋ mana?]
Which?	**Yang mana?**	[yaŋ mana?]
To whom?	**Kepada siapa?**	[kepada siapa?],
	Untuk siapa?	[untu' siapa?]
About whom?	**Tentang siapa?**	[tentaŋ siapa?]
About what?	**Tentang apa?**	[tentaŋ apa?]
With whom?	**Dengan siapa?**	[deŋan siapa?]
How many? How much?	**Berapa?**	[bərapa?]
Whose?	**Milik siapa?**	[mili' siapa?]

4. Prepositions

with (accompanied by)	**dengan**	[deŋan]
without	**tanpa**	[tanpa]
to (indicating direction)	**ke**	[ke]
about (talking ~ ...)	**tentang ...**	[tentaŋ ...]
before (in time)	**sebelum**	[sebelum]
in front of ...	**di depan ...**	[di depan ...]
under (beneath, below)	**di bawah**	[di bawah]
above (over)	**di atas**	[di atas]
on (atop)	**di atas**	[di atas]
from (off, out of)	**dari**	[dari]
of (made from)	**dari**	[dari]
in (e.g. ~ ten minutes)	**dalam**	[dalam]
over (across the top of)	**melalui**	[melalui]

5. Function words. Adverbs. Part 1

Where? (at, in)	**Di mana?**	[di mana?]
here (adv)	**di sini**	[di sini]
there (adv)	**di sana**	[di sana]
somewhere (to be)	**di suatu tempat**	[di suatu tempat]
nowhere (not in any place)	**tak ada di mana pun**	[taʾ ada di mana pun]
by (near, beside)	**dekat**	[dekat]
by the window	**dekat jendela**	[dekat dʒʲendela]
Where (to)?	**Ke mana?**	[ke mana?]
here (e.g. come ~!)	**ke sini**	[ke sini]
there (e.g. to go ~)	**ke sana**	[ke sana]
from here (adv)	**dari sini**	[dari sini]
from there (adv)	**dari sana**	[dari sana]
close (adv)	**dekat**	[dekat]
far (adv)	**jauh**	[dʒʲauh]
near (e.g. ~ Paris)	**dekat**	[dekat]
nearby (adv)	**dekat**	[dekat]
not far (adv)	**tidak jauh**	[tidaʾ dʒʲauh]
left (adj)	**kiri**	[kiri]
on the left	**di kiri**	[di kiri]
to the left	**ke kiri**	[ke kiri]
right (adj)	**kanan**	[kanan]
on the right	**di kanan**	[di kanan]
to the right	**ke kanan**	[ke kanan]
in front (adv)	**di depan**	[di depan]
front (as adj)	**depan**	[depan]
ahead (the kids ran ~)	**ke depan**	[ke depan]
behind (adv)	**di belakang**	[di belakaŋ]
from behind	**dari belakang**	[dari belakaŋ]
back (towards the rear)	**mundur**	[mundur]
middle	**tengah**	[teŋah]
in the middle	**di tengah**	[di teŋah]
at the side	**di sisi, di samping**	[di sisi], [di sampiŋ]
everywhere (adv)	**di mana-mana**	[di mana-mana]
around (in all directions)	**di sekitar**	[di sekitar]
from inside	**dari dalam**	[dari dalam]
somewhere (to go)	**ke suatu tempat**	[ke suatu tempat]
straight (directly)	**terus**	[terus]
back (e.g. come ~)	**kembali**	[kembali]
from anywhere	**dari mana pun**	[dari mana pun]
from somewhere	**dari suatu tempat**	[dari suatu tempat]

firstly (adv)	pertama	[pərtama]
secondly (adv)	kedua	[kedua]
thirdly (adv)	ketiga	[ketiga]

suddenly (adv)	tiba-tiba	[tiba-tiba]
at first (in the beginning)	mula-mula	[mula-mula]
for the first time	untuk pertama kalinya	[untu' pərtama kalinja]
long before ...	jauh sebelum ...	[dʒ'auh sebelum ...]
anew (over again)	kembali	[kembali]
for good (adv)	untuk selama-lamanya	[untu' selama-lamanja]

never (adv)	tidak pernah	[tida' pərnah]
again (adv)	lagi, kembali	[lagi], [kembali]
now (at present)	sekarang	[sekaraŋ]
often (adv)	sering, seringkali	[seriŋ], [seriŋkali]
then (adv)	ketika itu	[ketika itu]
urgently (quickly)	segera	[segera]
usually (adv)	biasanya	[biasanja]

by the way, ...	ngomong-ngomong ...	[ŋomoŋ-ŋomoŋ ...]
possibly	mungkin	[muŋkin]
probably (adv)	mungkin	[muŋkin]
maybe (adv)	mungkin	[muŋkin]
besides ...	selain itu ...	[selajn itu ...]
that's why ...	karena itu ...	[karena itu ...]
in spite of ...	meskipun ...	[meskipun ...]
thanks to ...	berkat ...	[berkat ...]

what (pron.)	apa	[apa]
that (conj.)	bahwa	[bahwa]
something	sesuatu	[sesuatu]
anything (something)	sesuatu	[sesuatu]
nothing	tidak sesuatu pun	[tida' sesuatu pun]

who (pron.)	siapa	[siapa]
someone	seseorang	[seseoraŋ]
somebody	seseorang	[seseoraŋ]

nobody	tidak seorang pun	[tida' seoraŋ pun]
nowhere (a voyage to ~)	tidak ke mana pun	[tida' ke mana pun]
nobody's	tidak milik siapa pun	[tida' mili' siapa pun]
somebody's	milik seseorang	[mili' seseoraŋ]

so (I'm ~ glad)	sangat	[saŋat]
also (as well)	juga	[dʒ'uga]
too (as well)	juga	[dʒ'uga]

6. Function words. Adverbs. Part 2

Why?	Mengapa?	[məŋapa?]
for some reason	entah mengapa	[entah məŋapa]
because ...	karena ...	[karena ...]
for some purpose	untuk tujuan tertentu	[untu' tudʒ'uan tertentu]
and	dan	[dan]

or	**atau**	[atau]
but	**tetapi, namun**	[tetapi], [namun]
for (e.g. ~ me)	**untuk**	[untuʔ]

too (excessively)	**terlalu**	[tərlalu]
only (exclusively)	**hanya**	[hanja]
exactly (adv)	**tepat**	[tepat]
about (more or less)	**sekitar**	[sekitar]

approximately (adv)	**kira-kira**	[kira-kira]
approximate (adj)	**kira-kira**	[kira-kira]
almost (adv)	**hampir**	[hampir]
the rest	**selebihnya, sisanya**	[selebihnja], [sisanja]

the other (second)	**kedua**	[kedua]
other (different)	**lain**	[lain]
each (adj)	**setiap**	[setiap]
any (no matter which)	**sebarang**	[sebaraŋ]
many, much (a lot of)	**banyak**	[banjaʔ]
many people	**banyak orang**	[banjaʔ oraŋ]
all (everyone)	**semua**	[semua]

in return for …	**sebagai ganti …**	[sebagaj ganti …]
in exchange (adv)	**sebagai gantinya**	[sebagaj gantinja]
by hand (made)	**dengan tangan**	[deŋan taŋan]
hardly (negative opinion)	**hampir tidak**	[hampir tidaʔ]

probably (adv)	**mungkin**	[muŋkin]
on purpose (intentionally)	**sengaja**	[seŋadʒʲa]
by accident (adv)	**tidak sengaja**	[tidaʔ seŋadʒʲa]

very (adv)	**sangat**	[saŋat]
for example (adv)	**misalnya**	[misalnja]
between	**antara**	[antara]
among	**di antara**	[di antara]
so much (such a lot)	**banyak sekali**	[banjaʔ sekali]
especially (adv)	**terutama**	[tərutama]

NUMBERS. MISCELLANEOUS

7. Cardinal numbers. Part 1

0 zero	nol	[nol]
1 one	satu	[satu]
2 two	dua	[dua]
3 three	tiga	[tiga]
4 four	empat	[empat]
5 five	lima	[lima]
6 six	enam	[enam]
7 seven	tujuh	[tudʒʲuh]
8 eight	delapan	[delapan]
9 nine	sembilan	[sembilan]
10 ten	sepuluh	[sepuluh]
11 eleven	sebelas	[sebelas]
12 twelve	dua belas	[dua belas]
13 thirteen	tiga belas	[tiga belas]
14 fourteen	empat belas	[empat belas]
15 fifteen	lima belas	[lima belas]
16 sixteen	enam belas	[enam belas]
17 seventeen	tujuh belas	[tudʒʲuh belas]
18 eighteen	delapan belas	[delapan belas]
19 nineteen	sembilan belas	[sembilan belas]
20 twenty	dua puluh	[dua puluh]
21 twenty-one	dua puluh satu	[dua puluh satu]
22 twenty-two	dua puluh dua	[dua puluh dua]
23 twenty-three	dua puluh tiga	[dua puluh tiga]
30 thirty	tiga puluh	[tiga puluh]
31 thirty-one	tiga puluh satu	[tiga puluh satu]
32 thirty-two	tiga puluh dua	[tiga puluh dua]
33 thirty-three	tiga puluh tiga	[tiga puluh tiga]
40 forty	empat puluh	[empat puluh]
41 forty-one	empat puluh satu	[empat puluh satu]
42 forty-two	empat puluh dua	[empat puluh dua]
43 forty-three	empat puluh tiga	[empat puluh tiga]
50 fifty	lima puluh	[lima puluh]
51 fifty-one	lima puluh satu	[lima puluh satu]
52 fifty-two	lima puluh dua	[lima puluh dua]
53 fifty-three	lima puluh tiga	[lima puluh tiga]
60 sixty	enam puluh	[enam puluh]
61 sixty-one	enam puluh satu	[enam puluh satu]

62 sixty-two	**enam puluh dua**	[enam puluh dua]
63 sixty-three	**enam puluh tiga**	[enam puluh tiga]
70 seventy	**tujuh puluh**	[tudʒʲuh puluh]
71 seventy-one	**tujuh puluh satu**	[tudʒʲuh puluh satu]
72 seventy-two	**tujuh puluh dua**	[tudʒʲuh puluh dua]
73 seventy-three	**tujuh puluh tiga**	[tudʒʲuh puluh tiga]
80 eighty	**delapan puluh**	[delapan puluh]
81 eighty-one	**delapan puluh satu**	[delapan puluh satu]
82 eighty-two	**delapan puluh dua**	[delapan puluh dua]
83 eighty-three	**delapan puluh tiga**	[delapan puluh tiga]
90 ninety	**sembilan puluh**	[sembilan puluh]
91 ninety-one	**sembulan puluh satu**	[sembulan puluh satu]
92 ninety-two	**sembilan puluh dua**	[sembilan puluh dua]
93 ninety-three	**sembilan puluh tiga**	[sembilan puluh tiga]

8. Cardinal numbers. Part 2

100 one hundred	**seratus**	[seratus]
200 two hundred	**dua ratus**	[dua ratus]
300 three hundred	**tiga ratus**	[tiga ratus]
400 four hundred	**empat ratus**	[empat ratus]
500 five hundred	**lima ratus**	[lima ratus]
600 six hundred	**enam ratus**	[enam ratus]
700 seven hundred	**tujuh ratus**	[tudʒʲuh ratus]
800 eight hundred	**delapan ratus**	[delapan ratus]
900 nine hundred	**sembilan ratus**	[sembilan ratus]
1000 one thousand	**seribu**	[seribu]
2000 two thousand	**dua ribu**	[dua ribu]
3000 three thousand	**tiga ribu**	[tiga ribu]
10000 ten thousand	**sepuluh ribu**	[sepuluh ribu]
one hundred thousand	**seratus ribu**	[seratus ribu]
million	**juta**	[dʒʲuta]
billion	**miliar**	[miliar]

9. Ordinal numbers

first (adj)	**pertama**	[pertama]
second (adj)	**kedua**	[kedua]
third (adj)	**ketiga**	[ketiga]
fourth (adj)	**keempat**	[keempat]
fifth (adj)	**kelima**	[kelima]
sixth (adj)	**keenam**	[keenam]
seventh (adj)	**ketujuh**	[ketudʒʲuh]
eighth (adj)	**kedelapan**	[kedelapan]
ninth (adj)	**kesembilan**	[kesembilan]
tenth (adj)	**kesepuluh**	[kesepuluh]

COLORS. UNITS OF MEASUREMENT

10. Colours

colour	**warna**	[warna]
shade (tint)	**nuansa**	[nuansa]
hue	**warna**	[warna]
rainbow	**pelangi**	[pelaŋi]
white (adj)	**putih**	[putih]
black (adj)	**hitam**	[hitam]
grey (adj)	**kelabu**	[kelabu]
green (adj)	**hijau**	[hidʒⁱau]
yellow (adj)	**kuning**	[kuniŋ]
red (adj)	**merah**	[merah]
blue (adj)	**biru**	[biru]
light blue (adj)	**biru muda**	[biru muda]
pink (adj)	**pink**	[pin']
orange (adj)	**oranye, jingga**	[oranje], [dʒiŋga]
violet (adj)	**violet, ungu muda**	[violet], [uŋu muda]
brown (adj)	**cokelat**	[tʃokelat]
golden (adj)	**keemasan**	[keemasan]
silvery (adj)	**keperakan**	[keperakan]
beige (adj)	**abu-abu kecokelatan**	[abu-abu ketʃokelatan]
cream (adj)	**krem**	[krem]
turquoise (adj)	**pirus**	[pirus]
cherry red (adj)	**merah tua**	[merah tua]
lilac (adj)	**ungu**	[uŋu]
crimson (adj)	**merah lembayung**	[merah lembajuŋ]
light (adj)	**terang**	[teraŋ]
dark (adj)	**gelap**	[gelap]
bright, vivid (adj)	**terang**	[teraŋ]
coloured (pencils)	**berwarna**	[bərwarna]
colour (e.g. ~ film)	**warna**	[warna]
black-and-white (adj)	**hitam-putih**	[hitam-putih]
plain (one-coloured)	**polos, satu warna**	[polos], [satu warna]
multicoloured (adj)	**berwarna-warni**	[bərwarna-warni]

11. Units of measurement

weight	**berat**	[berat]
length	**panjang**	[pandʒⁱaŋ]

width	**lebar**	[lebar]
height	**ketinggian**	[ketiŋgian]
depth	**kedalaman**	[kedalaman]
volume	**volume, isi**	[volume], [isi]
area	**luas**	[luas]
gram	**gram**	[gram]
milligram	**miligram**	[miligram]
kilogram	**kilogram**	[kilogram]
ton	**ton**	[ton]
pound	**pon**	[pon]
ounce	**ons**	[ons]
metre	**meter**	[meter]
millimetre	**milimeter**	[milimeter]
centimetre	**sentimeter**	[sentimeter]
kilometre	**kilometer**	[kilometer]
mile	**mil**	[mil]
inch	**inci**	[intʃi]
foot	**kaki**	[kaki]
yard	**yard**	[yard]
square metre	**meter persegi**	[meter pərsegi]
hectare	**hektar**	[hektar]
litre	**liter**	[liter]
degree	**derajat**	[deradʒiat]
volt	**volt**	[volt]
ampere	**ampere**	[ampere]
horsepower	**tenaga kuda**	[tenaga kuda]
quantity	**kuantitas**	[kuantitas]
a little bit of ...	**sedikit ...**	[sedikit ...]
half	**setengah**	[seteŋah]
dozen	**lusin**	[lusin]
piece (item)	**buah**	[buah]
size	**ukuran**	[ukuran]
scale (map ~)	**skala**	[skala]
minimal (adj)	**minimal**	[minimal]
the smallest (adj)	**terkecil**	[tərketʃil]
medium (adj)	**sedang**	[sedaŋ]
maximal (adj)	**maksimal**	[maksimal]
the largest (adj)	**terbesar**	[tərbesar]

12. Containers

canning jar (glass ~)	**gelas**	[gelas]
tin, can	**kaleng**	[kaleŋ]
bucket	**ember**	[ember]
barrel	**tong**	[toŋ]
wash basin (e.g., plastic ~)	**baskom**	[baskom]

tank (100L water ~)	tangki	[taŋki]
hip flask	pelples	[pelples]
jerrycan	jeriken	[dʒ'eriken]
tank (e.g., tank car)	tangki	[taŋki]

mug	mangkuk	[maŋkuʔ]
cup (of coffee, etc.)	cangkir	[tʃaŋkir]
saucer	alas cangkir	[alas tʃaŋkir]
glass (tumbler)	gelas	[gelas]
wine glass	gelas anggur	[gelas aŋgur]
stock pot (soup pot)	panci	[pantʃi]

| bottle (~ of wine) | botol | [botol] |
| neck (of the bottle, etc.) | leher | [leher] |

carafe (decanter)	karaf	[karaf]
pitcher	kendi	[kendi]
vessel (container)	wadah	[wadah]
pot (crock, stoneware ~)	pot	[pot]
vase	vas	[vas]

flacon, bottle (perfume ~)	botol	[botol]
vial, small bottle	botol kecil	[botol ketʃil]
tube (of toothpaste)	tabung	[tabuŋ]

sack (bag)	karung	[karuŋ]
bag (paper ~, plastic ~)	kantong	[kantoŋ]
packet (of cigarettes, etc.)	bungkus	[buŋkus]

box (e.g. shoebox)	kotak, kardus	[kotak], [kardus]
crate	kotak	[kotaʔ]
basket	bakul	[bakul]

MAIN VERBS

to advise (vt)	menasihati	[mənasihati]
to agree (say yes)	setuju	[setudʒiu]
to answer (vi, vt)	menjawab	[məndʒiawab]
to apologize (vi)	meminta maaf	[meminta ma'af]
to arrive (vi)	datang	[dataŋ]
to ask (~ oneself)	bertanya	[bərtanja]
to ask (~ sb to do sth)	meminta	[meminta]
to be (~ a teacher)	ialah, adalah	[ialah], [adalah]
to be (~ on a diet)	sedang	[sedaŋ]
to be afraid	takut	[takut]
to be hungry	lapar	[lapar]
to be interested in …	menaruh minat pada …	[mənaruh minat pada …]
to be needed	dibutuhkan	[dibutuhkan]
to be surprised	heran	[heran]
to be thirsty	haus	[haus]
to begin (vt)	memulai, membuka	[memulaj], [membuka]
to belong to …	kepunyaan …	[kepunja'an …]
to boast (vi)	membual	[membual]
to break (split into pieces)	memecahkan	[memetʃahkan]
to call (~ for help)	memanggil	[memaŋgil]
can (v aux)	bisa	[bisa]
to catch (vt)	menangkap	[mənaŋkap]
to change (vt)	mengubah	[məŋubah]
to choose (select)	memilih	[memilih]
to come down (the stairs)	turun	[turun]
to compare (vt)	membandingkan	[membandiŋkan]
to complain (vi, vt)	mengeluh	[məŋeluh]
to confuse (mix up)	bingung membedakan	[biŋuŋ membedakan]
to continue (vt)	meneruskan	[məneruskan]
to control (vt)	mengontrol	[məŋontrol]
to cook (dinner)	memasak	[memasaʔ]
to cost (vt)	berharga	[bərharga]
to count (add up)	menghitung	[məŋhituŋ]
to count on …	mengharapkan …	[məŋharapkan …]
to create (vt)	menciptakan	[mentʃiptakan]
to cry (weep)	menangis	[mənaŋis]

14. The most important verbs. Part 2

to deceive (vi, vt)	menipu	[mənipu]
to decorate (tree, street)	menghiasi	[məŋhiasi]
to defend (a country, etc.)	membela	[membela]
to demand (request firmly)	menuntut	[mənuntut]
to dig (vt)	menggali	[məŋgali]
to discuss (vt)	membicarakan	[membitʃarakan]
to do (vt)	membuat	[membuat]
to doubt (have doubts)	ragu-ragu	[ragu-ragu]
to drop (let fall)	tercecer	[tərtʃetʃer]
to enter (room, house, etc.)	masuk, memasuki	[masuk], [memasuki]
to excuse (forgive)	memaafkan	[memaʔafkan]
to exist (vi)	ada	[ada]
to expect (foresee)	menduga	[mənduga]
to explain (vt)	menjelaskan	[məndʒelaskan]
to fall (vi)	jatuh	[dʒatuh]
to fancy (vt)	suka	[suka]
to find (vt)	menemukan	[mənemukan]
to finish (vt)	mengakhiri	[məŋahiri]
to fly (vi)	terbang	[tərbaŋ]
to follow ... (come after)	mengikuti ...	[məŋikuti ...]
to forget (vi, vt)	melupakan	[melupakan]
to forgive (vt)	memaafkan	[memaʔafkan]
to give (vt)	memberi	[memberi]
to give a hint	memberi petunjuk	[memberi petundʒuʔ]
to go (on foot)	berjalan	[bərdʒalan]
to go for a swim	berenang	[bərenaŋ]
to go out (for dinner, etc.)	keluar	[keluar]
to guess (the answer)	menerka	[mənerka]
to have (vt)	mempunyai	[mempunjaj]
to have breakfast	sarapan	[sarapan]
to have dinner	makan malam	[makan malam]
to have lunch	makan siang	[makan siaŋ]
to hear (vt)	mendengar	[məndeŋar]
to help (vt)	membantu	[membantu]
to hide (vt)	menyembunyikan	[mənjembunjikan]
to hope (vi, vt)	berharap	[bərharap]
to hunt (vi, vt)	berburu	[bərburu]
to hurry (vi)	tergesa-gesa	[tərgesa-gesa]

15. The most important verbs. Part 3

to inform (vt)	menginformasikan	[mənjinformasikan]
to insist (vi, vt)	mendesak	[məndesaʔ]
to insult (vt)	menghina	[mənhina]

to invite (vt)	mengundang	[məŋundaŋ]
to joke (vi)	bergurau	[bərgurau]
to keep (vt)	menyimpan	[mənjimpan]
to keep silent, to hush	diam	[diam]
to kill (vt)	membunuh	[membunuh]
to know (sb)	kenal	[kenal]
to know (sth)	tahu	[tahu]
to laugh (vi)	tertawa	[tərtawa]
to liberate (city, etc.)	membebaskan	[membebaskan]
to look for … (search)	mencari …	[məntʃari …]
to love (sb)	mencintai	[məntʃintaj]
to make a mistake	salah	[salah]
to manage, to run	memimpin	[memimpin]
to mean (signify)	berarti	[bərarti]
to mention (talk about)	menyebut	[mənjebut]
to miss (school, etc.)	absen	[absen]
to notice (see)	memperhatikan	[memperhatikan]
to object (vi, vt)	keberatan	[keberatan]
to observe (see)	mengamati	[məŋamati]
to open (vt)	membuka	[membuka]
to order (meal, etc.)	memesan	[memesan]
to order (mil.)	memerintahkan	[memerintahkan]
to own (possess)	memiliki	[memiliki]
to participate (vi)	turut serta	[turut serta]
to pay (vi, vt)	membayar	[membajar]
to permit (vt)	mengizinkan	[məŋizinkan]
to plan (vt)	merencanakan	[merentʃanakan]
to play (children)	bermain	[bərmajn]
to pray (vi, vt)	bersembahyang, berdoa	[bərsembahjaŋ], [bərdoa]
to prefer (vt)	lebih suka	[lebih suka]
to promise (vt)	berjanji	[bərdʒ'andʒi]
to pronounce (vt)	melafalkan	[melafalkan]
to propose (vt)	mengusulkan	[məŋusulkan]
to punish (vt)	menghukum	[məŋhukum]

16. The most important verbs. Part 4

to read (vi, vt)	membaca	[membatʃa]
to recommend (vt)	merekomendasi	[merekomendasi]
to refuse (vi, vt)	menolak	[mənola']
to regret (be sorry)	menyesal	[mənjesal]
to rent (sth from sb)	menyewa	[mənjewa]
to repeat (say again)	mengulangi	[məŋulaŋi]
to reserve, to book	memesan	[memesan]
to run (vi)	lari	[lari]
to save (rescue)	menyelamatkan	[mənjelamatkan]
to say (~ thank you)	berkata	[bərkata]

to scold (vt)	memarahi, menegur	[memarahi], [menegur]
to see (vt)	melihat	[melihat]
to sell (vt)	menjual	[məndʒ'ual]
to send (vt)	mengirim	[məɲirim]
to shoot (vi)	menembak	[mənembaʔ]
to shout (vi)	berteriak	[bərteriaʔ]
to show (vt)	menunjukkan	[mənundʒ'uʔkan]
to sign (document)	menandatangani	[mənandataŋani]
to sit down (vi)	duduk	[duduʔ]
to smile (vi)	tersenyum	[tərsenyum]
to speak (vi, vt)	berbicara	[bərbitʃara]
to steal (money, etc.)	mencuri	[məntʃuri]
to stop (for pause, etc.)	berhenti	[bərhenti]
to stop (please ~ calling me)	menghentikan	[məŋhentikan]
to study (vt)	mempelajari	[mempeladʒ'ari]
to swim (vi)	berenang	[bərenaŋ]
to take (vt)	mengambil	[məŋambil]
to think (vi, vt)	berpikir	[bərpikir]
to threaten (vt)	mengancam	[məŋantʃam]
to touch (with hands)	menyentuh	[mənjentuh]
to translate (vt)	menerjemahkan	[mənerdʒ'emahkan]
to trust (vt)	mempercayai	[mempertʃajaj]
to try (attempt)	mencoba	[məntʃoba]
to turn (e.g., ~ left)	membelok	[membeloʔ]
to underestimate (vt)	meremehkan	[meremehkan]
to understand (vt)	mengerti	[məŋerti]
to unite (vt)	menyatukan	[mənjatukan]
to wait (vt)	menunggu	[mənuŋgu]
to want (wish, desire)	mau, ingin	[mau], [iɲin]
to warn (vt)	memperingatkan	[memperiŋatkan]
to work (vi)	bekerja	[bekerdʒ'a]
to write (vt)	menulis	[mənulis]
to write down	mencatat	[məntʃatat]

TIME. CALENDAR

17. Weekdays

Monday	**Hari Senin**	[hari senin]
Tuesday	**Hari Selasa**	[hari selasa]
Wednesday	**Hari Rabu**	[hari rabu]
Thursday	**Hari Kamis**	[hari kamis]
Friday	**Hari Jumat**	[hari dʒˈumat]
Saturday	**Hari Sabtu**	[hari sabtu]
Sunday	**Hari Minggu**	[hari miŋgu]
today (adv)	**hari ini**	[hari ini]
tomorrow (adv)	**besok**	[besoʔ]
the day after tomorrow	**besok lusa**	[besoʔ lusa]
yesterday (adv)	**kemarin**	[kemarin]
the day before yesterday	**kemarin dulu**	[kemarin dulu]
day	**hari**	[hari]
working day	**hari kerja**	[hari kerdʒˈa]
public holiday	**hari libur**	[hari libur]
day off	**hari libur**	[hari libur]
weekend	**akhir pekan**	[ahir pekan]
all day long	**seharian**	[seharian]
the next day (adv)	**hari berikutnya**	[hari berikutnja]
two days ago	**dua hari lalu**	[dua hari lalu]
the day before	**hari sebelumnya**	[hari sebelumnja]
daily (adj)	**harian**	[harian]
every day (adv)	**tiap hari**	[tiap hari]
week	**minggu**	[miŋgu]
last week (adv)	**minggu lalu**	[miŋgu lalu]
next week (adv)	**minggu berikutnya**	[miŋgu berikutnja]
weekly (adj)	**mingguan**	[miŋguan]
every week (adv)	**tiap minggu**	[tiap miŋgu]
twice a week	**dua kali seminggu**	[dua kali semiŋgu]
every Tuesday	**tiap Hari Selasa**	[tiap hari selasa]

18. Hours. Day and night

morning	**pagi**	[pagi]
in the morning	**pada pagi hari**	[pada pagi hari]
noon, midday	**tengah hari**	[teŋah hari]
in the afternoon	**pada sore hari**	[pada sore hari]
evening	**sore, malam**	[sore], [malam]
in the evening	**waktu sore**	[waktu sore]

night	**malam**	[malam]
at night	**pada malam hari**	[pada malam hari]
midnight	**tengah malam**	[teŋah malam]

second	**detik**	[deti']
minute	**menit**	[menit]
hour	**jam**	[dʒʲam]
half an hour	**setengah jam**	[seteŋah dʒʲam]
a quarter-hour	**seperempat jam**	[seperempat dʒʲam]
fifteen minutes	**lima belas menit**	[lima belas menit]
24 hours	**siang-malam**	[siaŋ-malam]

sunrise	**matahari terbit**	[matahari tərbit]
dawn	**subuh**	[subuh]
early morning	**dini pagi**	[dini pagi]
sunset	**matahari terbenam**	[matahari tərbenam]

early in the morning	**pagi-pagi**	[pagi-pagi]
this morning	**pagi ini**	[pagi ini]
tomorrow morning	**besok pagi**	[beso' pagi]

this afternoon	**sore ini**	[sore ini]
in the afternoon	**pada sore hari**	[pada sore hari]
tomorrow afternoon	**besok sore**	[beso' sore]

| tonight (this evening) | **sore ini** | [sore ini] |
| tomorrow night | **besok malam** | [beso' malam] |

at 3 o'clock sharp	**pukul 3 tepat**	[pukul tiga tepat]
about 4 o'clock	**sekitar pukul 4**	[sekitar pukul empat]
by 12 o'clock	**pada pukul 12**	[pada pukul belas]

in 20 minutes	**dalam 20 menit**	[dalam dua puluh menit]
in an hour	**dalam satu jam**	[dalam satu dʒʲam]
on time (adv)	**tepat waktu**	[tepat waktu]

a quarter to ...	**... kurang seperempat**	[... kuraŋ seperempat]
within an hour	**selama sejam**	[selama sedʒʲam]
every 15 minutes	**tiap 15 menit**	[tiap lima belas menit]
round the clock	**siang-malam**	[siaŋ-malam]

19. Months. Seasons

January	**Januari**	[dʒʲanuari]
February	**Februari**	[februari]
March	**Maret**	[maret]
April	**April**	[april]
May	**Mei**	[mei]
June	**Juni**	[dʒʲuni]

July	**Juli**	[dʒʲuli]
August	**Augustus**	[augustus]
September	**September**	[september]
October	**Oktober**	[oktober]

| November | **November** | [november] |
| December | **Desember** | [desember] |

spring	**musim semi**	[musim semi]
in spring	**pada musim semi**	[pada musim semi]
spring (as adj)	**musim semi**	[musim semi]

summer	**musim panas**	[musim panas]
in summer	**pada musim panas**	[pada musim panas]
summer (as adj)	**musim panas**	[musim panas]

autumn	**musim gugur**	[musim gugur]
in autumn	**pada musim gugur**	[pada musim gugur]
autumn (as adj)	**musim gugur**	[musim gugur]

winter	**musim dingin**	[musim diŋin]
in winter	**pada musim dingin**	[pada musim diŋin]
winter (as adj)	**musim dingin**	[musim diŋin]

month	**bulan**	[bulan]
this month	**bulan ini**	[bulan ini]
next month	**bulan depan**	[bulan depan]
last month	**bulan lalu**	[bulan lalu]

a month ago	**sebulan lalu**	[sebulan lalu]
in a month (a month later)	**dalam satu bulan**	[dalam satu bulan]
in 2 months (2 months later)	**dalam 2 bulan**	[dalam dua bulan]
the whole month	**sepanjang bulan**	[sepandʒʲaŋ bulan]
all month long	**sebulan penuh**	[sebulan penuh]

monthly (~ magazine)	**bulanan**	[bulanan]
monthly (adv)	**tiap bulan**	[tiap bulan]
every month	**tiap bulan**	[tiap bulan]
twice a month	**dua kali sebulan**	[dua kali sebulan]

year	**tahun**	[tahun]
this year	**tahun ini**	[tahun ini]
next year	**tahun depan**	[tahun depan]
last year	**tahun lalu**	[tahun lalu]

a year ago	**setahun lalu**	[setahun lalu]
in a year	**dalam satu tahun**	[dalam satu tahun]
in two years	**dalam 2 tahun**	[dalam dua tahun]
the whole year	**sepanjang tahun**	[sepandʒʲaŋ tahun]
all year long	**setahun penuh**	[setahun penuh]

every year	**tiap tahun**	[tiap tahun]
annual (adj)	**tahunan**	[tahunan]
annually (adv)	**tiap tahun**	[tiap tahun]
4 times a year	**empat kali setahun**	[empat kali setahun]

date (e.g. today's ~)	**tanggal**	[taŋgal]
date (e.g. ~ of birth)	**tanggal**	[taŋgal]
calendar	**kalender**	[kalender]
half a year	**setengah tahun**	[seteŋah tahun]
six months	**enam bulan**	[enam bulan]

season (summer, etc.)	**musim**	[musim]
century	**abad**	[abad]

TRAVEL. HOTEL

20. Trip. Travel

tourism, travel	**pariwisata**	[pariwisata]
tourist	**turis, wisatawan**	[turis], [wisatawan]
trip, voyage	**pengembaraan**	[peŋembara'an]
adventure	**petualangan**	[petualaŋan]
trip, journey	**perjalanan, lawatan**	[pərdʒ'alanan], [lawatan]
holiday	**liburan**	[liburan]
to be on holiday	**berlibur**	[bərlibur]
rest	**istirahat**	[istirahat]
train	**kereta api**	[kereta api]
by train	**naik kereta api**	[nai' kereta api]
aeroplane	**pesawat terbang**	[pesawat tərbaŋ]
by aeroplane	**naik pesawat terbang**	[nai' pesawat tərbaŋ]
by car	**naik mobil**	[nai' mobil]
by ship	**naik kapal**	[nai' kapal]
luggage	**bagasi**	[bagasi]
suitcase	**koper**	[koper]
luggage trolley	**troli bagasi**	[troli bagasi]
passport	**paspor**	[paspor]
visa	**visa**	[visa]
ticket	**tiket**	[tiket]
air ticket	**tiket pesawat terbang**	[tiket pesawat tərbaŋ]
guidebook	**buku pedoman**	[buku pedoman]
map (tourist ~)	**peta**	[peta]
area (rural ~)	**kawasan**	[kawasan]
place, site	**tempat**	[tempat]
exotica (n)	**keeksotisan**	[keeksotisan]
exotic (adj)	**eksotis**	[eksotis]
amazing (adj)	**menakjubkan**	[mənakdʒ'ubkan]
group	**kelompok**	[kelompo']
excursion, sightseeing tour	**ekskursi**	[ekskursi]
guide (person)	**pemandu wisata**	[pemandu wisata]

21. Hotel

hotel	**hotel**	[hotel]
motel	**motel**	[motel]
three-star (~ hotel)	**bintang tiga**	[bintaŋ tiga]

five-star	**bintang lima**	[bintaŋ lima]
to stay (in a hotel, etc.)	**menginap**	[məŋinap]
room	**kamar**	[kamar]
single room	**kamar tunggal**	[kamar tuŋgal]
double room	**kamar ganda**	[kamar ganda]
to book a room	**memesan kamar**	[memesan kamar]
half board	**sewa setengah**	[sewa seteŋah]
full board	**sewa penuh**	[sewa penuh]
with bath	**dengan kamar mandi**	[deŋan kamar mandi]
with shower	**dengan pancuran**	[deŋan pantʃuran]
satellite television	**televisi satelit**	[televisi satelit]
air-conditioner	**penyejuk udara**	[penjedʒ'u' udara]
towel	**handuk**	[handu']
key	**kunci**	[kuntʃi]
administrator	**administrator**	[administrator]
chambermaid	**pelayan kamar**	[pelajan kamar]
porter	**porter**	[porter]
doorman	**pramupintu**	[pramupintu]
restaurant	**restoran**	[restoran]
pub, bar	**bar**	[bar]
breakfast	**makan pagi, sarapan**	[makan pagi], [sarapan]
dinner	**makan malam**	[makan malam]
buffet	**prasmanan**	[prasmanan]
lobby	**lobi**	[lobi]
lift	**elevator**	[elevator]
DO NOT DISTURB	**JANGAN MENGGANGGU**	[dʒ'aŋan məŋgaŋu]
NO SMOKING	**DILARANG MEROKOK!**	[dilaraŋ meroko'!]

22. Sightseeing

monument	**monumen, patung**	[monumen], [patuŋ]
fortress	**benteng**	[benteŋ]
palace	**istana**	[istana]
castle	**kastil**	[kastil]
tower	**menara**	[mənara]
mausoleum	**mausoleum**	[mausoleum]
architecture	**arsitektur**	[arsitektur]
medieval (adj)	**abad pertengahan**	[abad perteŋahan]
ancient (adj)	**kuno**	[kuno]
national (adj)	**nasional**	[nasional]
famous (monument, etc.)	**terkenal**	[terkenal]
tourist	**turis, wisatawan**	[turis], [wisatawan]
guide (person)	**pemandu wisata**	[pemandu wisata]
excursion, sightseeing tour	**ekskursi**	[ekskursi]
to show (vt)	**menunjukkan**	[mənundʒ'u'kan]

to tell (vt)	**menceritakan**	[mənʧeritakan]
to find (vt)	**mendapatkan**	[məndapatkan]
to get lost (lose one's way)	**tersesat**	[tərsesat]
map (e.g. underground ~)	**denah**	[denah]
map (e.g. city ~)	**peta**	[peta]
souvenir, gift	**suvenir**	[suvenir]
gift shop	**toko suvenir**	[toko suvenir]
to take pictures	**memotret**	[memotret]
to have one's picture taken	**berfoto**	[bərfoto]

TRANSPORT

airport	bandara	[bandara]
aeroplane	pesawat terbang	[pesawat tərbaŋ]
airline	maskapai penerbangan	[maskapaj penerbaŋan]
air traffic controller	pengawas lalu lintas udara	[peŋawas lalu lintas udara]

departure	keberangkatan	[keberaŋkatan]
arrival	kedatangan	[kedataŋan]
to arrive (by plane)	datang	[dataŋ]

| departure time | waktu keberangkatan | [waktu keberaŋkatan] |
| arrival time | waktu kedatangan | [waktu kedataŋan] |

| to be delayed | terlambat | [tərlambat] |
| flight delay | penundaan penerbangan | [penunda'an penerbaŋan] |

information board	papan informasi	[papan informasi]
information	informasi	[informasi]
to announce (vt)	mengumumkan	[məŋumumkan]
flight (e.g. next ~)	penerbangan	[penerbaŋan]

| customs | pabean | [pabean] |
| customs officer | petugas pabean | [petugas pabean] |

customs declaration	pernyataan pabean	[pərnjata'an pabean]
to fill in (vt)	mengisi	[məŋisi]
to fill in the declaration	mengisi formulir bea cukai	[məŋisi formulir bea tʃukaj]
passport control	pemeriksaan paspor	[pemeriksa'an paspor]

luggage	bagasi	[bagasi]
hand luggage	jinjingan	[dʒindʒiŋan]
luggage trolley	troli bagasi	[troli bagasi]

landing	pendaratan	[pendaratan]
landing strip	jalur pendaratan	[dʒʲalur pendaratan]
to land (vi)	mendarat	[mendarat]
airstair (passenger stair)	tangga pesawat	[taŋga pesawat]

check-in	check-in	[tʃekin]
check-in counter	meja check-in	[medʒʲa tʃekin]
to check-in (vi)	check-in	[tʃekin]
boarding card	kartu pas	[kartu pas]
departure gate	gerbang keberangkatan	[gerbaŋ keberaŋkatan]

transit	transit	[transit]
to wait (vt)	menunggu	[mənuŋgu]
departure lounge	ruang tunggu	[ruaŋ tuŋgu]

| to see off | mengantar | [məŋantar] |
| to say goodbye | berpamitan | [bərpamitan] |

24. Aeroplane

aeroplane	pesawat terbang	[pesawat tərbaŋ]
air ticket	tiket pesawat terbang	[tiket pesawat tərbaŋ]
airline	maskapai penerbangan	[maskapaj penerbaŋan]
airport	bandara	[bandara]
supersonic (adj)	supersonik	[supersoni']

captain	kapten	[kapten]
crew	awak	[awa']
pilot	pilot	[pilot]
stewardess	pramugari	[pramugari]
navigator	navigator, penavigasi	[navigator], [penavigasi]

wings	sayap	[sajap]
tail	ekor	[ekor]
cockpit	kokpit	[kokpit]
engine	mesin	[mesin]
undercarriage (landing gear)	roda pendarat	[roda pendarat]
turbine	turbin	[turbin]
propeller	baling-baling	[baliŋ-baliŋ]
black box	kotak hitam	[kota' hitam]
yoke (control column)	kemudi	[kemudi]
fuel	bahan bakar	[bahan bakar]

safety card	instruksi keselamatan	[instruksi keselamatan]
oxygen mask	masker oksigen	[masker oksigen]
uniform	seragam	[seragam]
lifejacket	jaket pelampung	[dʒjaket pelampuŋ]
parachute	parasut	[parasut]
takeoff	lepas landas	[lepas landas]
to take off (vi)	bertolak	[bertola']
runway	jalur lepas landas	[dʒjalur lepas landas]

visibility	visibilitas, pandangan	[visibilitas], [pandaŋan]
flight (act of flying)	penerbangan	[penerbaŋan]
altitude	ketinggian	[ketiŋgian]
air pocket	lubang udara	[lubaŋ udara]

seat	tempat duduk	[tempat dudu']
headphones	headphone, fonkepala	[headphone], [fonkepala]
folding tray (tray table)	meja lipat	[medʒja lipat]
airplane window	jendela pesawat	[dʒjendela pesawat]
aisle	lorong	[loroŋ]

25. Train

| train | kereta api | [kereta api] |
| commuter train | kereta api listrik | [kereta api listri'] |

express train	**kereta api cepat**	[kereta api ʧepat]
diesel locomotive	**lokomotif diesel**	[lokomotif disel]
steam locomotive	**lokomotif uap**	[lokomotif uap]
coach, carriage	**gerbong penumpang**	[gerboŋ penumpaŋ]
buffet car	**gerbong makan**	[gerboŋ makan]
rails	**rel**	[rel]
railway	**rel kereta api**	[rel kereta api]
sleeper (track support)	**bantalan rel**	[bantalan rel]
platform (railway ~)	**platform**	[platform]
platform (~ 1, 2, etc.)	**jalur**	[dʒˈalur]
semaphore	**semafor**	[semafor]
station	**stasiun**	[stasiun]
train driver	**masinis**	[masinis]
porter (of luggage)	**porter**	[porter]
carriage attendant	**kondektur**	[kondektur]
passenger	**penumpang**	[penumpaŋ]
ticket inspector	**kondektur**	[kondektur]
corridor (in train)	**koridor**	[koridor]
emergency brake	**rem darurat**	[rem darurat]
compartment	**kabin**	[kabin]
berth	**bangku**	[baŋku]
upper berth	**bangku atas**	[baŋku atas]
lower berth	**bangku bawah**	[baŋku bawah]
bed linen, bedding	**kain kasur**	[kain kasur]
ticket	**tiket**	[tiket]
timetable	**jadwal**	[dʒˈadwal]
information display	**layar informasi**	[lajar informasi]
to leave, to depart	**berangkat**	[bəraŋkat]
departure (of a train)	**keberangkatan**	[keberaŋkatan]
to arrive (ab. train)	**datang**	[dataŋ]
arrival	**kedatangan**	[kedataŋan]
to arrive by train	**datang naik kereta api**	[dataŋ najˀ kereta api]
to get on the train	**naik ke kereta**	[naiˀ ke kereta]
to get off the train	**turun dari kereta**	[turun dari kereta]
train crash	**kecelakaan kereta**	[keʧelakaˀan kereta]
to derail (vi)	**keluar rel**	[keluar rel]
steam locomotive	**lokomotif uap**	[lokomotif uap]
stoker, fireman	**juru api**	[dʒˈuru api]
firebox	**tungku**	[tuŋku]
coal	**batu bara**	[batu bara]

26. Ship

ship	**kapal**	[kapal]
vessel	**kapal**	[kapal]

steamship	**kapal uap**	[kapal uap]
riverboat	**kapal api**	[kapal api]
cruise ship	**kapal laut**	[kapal laut]
cruiser	**kapal penjelajah**	[kapal pendʒˈeladʒˈah]
yacht	**perahu pesiar**	[pərahu pesiar]
tugboat	**kapal tunda**	[kapal tunda]
barge	**tongkang**	[toŋkaŋ]
ferry	**feri**	[feri]
sailing ship	**kapal layar**	[kapal lajar]
brigantine	**kapal brigantin**	[kapal brigantin]
ice breaker	**kapal pemecah es**	[kapal pemetʃah es]
submarine	**kapal selam**	[kapal selam]
boat (flat-bottomed ~)	**perahu**	[pərahu]
dinghy (lifeboat)	**sekoci**	[sekotʃi]
lifeboat	**sekoci penyelamat**	[sekotʃi penjelamat]
motorboat	**perahu motor**	[pərahu motor]
captain	**kapten**	[kapten]
seaman	**kelasi**	[kelasi]
sailor	**pelaut**	[pelaut]
crew	**awak**	[awaʔ]
boatswain	**bosman, bosun**	[bosman], [bosun]
ship's boy	**kadet laut**	[kadet laut]
cook	**koki**	[koki]
ship's doctor	**dokter kapal**	[dokter kapal]
deck	**dek**	[deʔ]
mast	**tiang**	[tiaŋ]
sail	**layar**	[lajar]
hold	**lambung kapal**	[lambuŋ kapal]
bow (prow)	**haluan**	[haluan]
stern	**buritan**	[buritan]
oar	**dayung**	[dajuŋ]
screw propeller	**baling-baling**	[baliŋ-baliŋ]
cabin	**kabin**	[kabin]
wardroom	**ruang rekreasi**	[ruaŋ rekreasi]
engine room	**ruang mesin**	[ruaŋ mesin]
bridge	**anjungan kapal**	[andʒˈuŋan kapal]
radio room	**ruang radio**	[ruaŋ radio]
wave (radio)	**gelombang radio**	[gelombaŋ radio]
logbook	**buku harian kapal**	[buku harian kapal]
spyglass	**teropong**	[təropoŋ]
bell	**lonceng**	[lontʃeŋ]
flag	**bendera**	[bendera]
hawser (mooring ~)	**tali**	[tali]
knot (bowline, etc.)	**simpul**	[simpul]
deckrails	**pegangan**	[pegaŋan]

gangway	tangga kapal	[taŋga kapal]
anchor	jangkar	[dʒɪaŋkar]
to weigh anchor	mengangkat jangkar	[məŋaŋkat dʒɪaŋkar]
to drop anchor	menjatuhkan jangkar	[məndʒɪatuhkan dʒɪaŋkar]
anchor chain	rantai jangkar	[rantaj dʒɪaŋkar]

port (harbour)	pelabuhan	[pelabuhan]
quay, wharf	dermaga	[dermaga]
to berth (moor)	merapat	[merapat]
to cast off	bertolak	[bərtolaʔ]

trip, voyage	pengembaraan	[peŋembaraʔan]
cruise (sea trip)	pesiar	[pesiar]
course (route)	haluan	[haluan]
route (itinerary)	rute	[rute]

| shallows | beting | [betiŋ] |
| to run aground | kandas | [kandas] |

storm	badai	[badaj]
signal	sinyal	[sinjal]
to sink (vi)	tenggelam	[teŋgelam]
Man overboard!	Orang hanyut!	[oraŋ hanyut!]
SOS (distress signal)	SOS	[es-o-es]
ring buoy	pelampung penyelamat	[pelampuŋ penjelamat]

CITY

bus, coach	bus	[bus]
tram	trem	[trem]
trolleybus	bus listrik	[bus listriʔ]
route (bus ~)	trayek	[traeʔ]
number (e.g. bus ~)	nomor	[nomor]
to go by ...	naik ...	[naiʔ ...]
to get on (~ the bus)	naik	[naiʔ]
to get off ...	turun ...	[turun ...]
stop (e.g. bus ~)	halte, pemberhentian	[halte], [pemberhentian]
next stop	halte berikutnya	[halte berikutnja]
terminus	halte terakhir	[halte terahir]
timetable	jadwal	[dʒ¡adwal]
to wait (vt)	menunggu	[menungu]
ticket	tiket	[tiket]
fare	harga karcis	[harga kartʃis]
cashier (ticket seller)	kasir	[kasir]
ticket inspection	pemeriksaan tiket	[pemeriksaʔan tiket]
ticket inspector	kondektur	[kondektur]
to be late (for ...)	terlambat ...	[terlambat ...]
to miss (~ the train, etc.)	ketinggalan	[ketingalan]
to be in a hurry	tergesa-gesa	[tergesa-gesa]
taxi, cab	taksi	[taksi]
taxi driver	sopir taksi	[sopir taksi]
by taxi	naik taksi	[naiʔ taksi]
taxi rank	pangkalan taksi	[pankalan taksi]
to call a taxi	memanggil taksi	[memangil taksi]
to take a taxi	menaiki taksi	[menajki taksi]
traffic	lalu lintas	[lalu lintas]
traffic jam	kemacetan lalu lintas	[kematʃetan lalu lintas]
rush hour	jam sibuk	[dʒ¡am sibuʔ]
to park (vi)	parkir	[parkir]
to park (vt)	memarkir	[memarkir]
car park	tempat parkir	[tempat parkir]
underground, tube	kereta api bawah tanah	[kereta api bawah tanah]
station	stasiun	[stasiun]
to take the tube	naik kereta api bawah tanah	[naiʔ kereta api bawah tanah]
train	kereta api	[kereta api]
train station	stasiun kereta api	[stasiun kereta api]

28. City. Life in the city

city, town	**kota**	[kota]
capital city	**ibu kota**	[ibu kota]
village	**desa**	[desa]
city map	**peta kota**	[peta kota]
city centre	**pusat kota**	[pusat kota]
suburb	**pinggir kota**	[piŋgir kota]
suburban (adj)	**pinggir kota**	[piŋgir kota]
outskirts	**pinggir**	[piŋgir]
environs (suburbs)	**daerah sekitarnya**	[daerah sekitarnja]
city block	**blok**	[blo']
residential block (area)	**blok perumahan**	[blo' perumahan]
traffic	**lalu lintas**	[lalu lintas]
traffic lights	**lampu lalu lintas**	[lampu lalu lintas]
public transport	**angkot**	[aŋkot]
crossroads	**persimpangan**	[persimpaŋan]
zebra crossing	**penyeberangan**	[penjeberaŋan]
pedestrian subway	**terowongan penyeberangan**	[terowoŋan penjeberaŋan]
to cross (~ the street)	**menyeberang**	[menjeberaŋ]
pedestrian	**pejalan kaki**	[pedʒalan kaki]
pavement	**trotoar**	[trotoar]
bridge	**jembatan**	[dʒembatan]
embankment (river walk)	**tepi sungai**	[tepi suŋaj]
fountain	**air mancur**	[air mantʃur]
allée (garden walkway)	**jalan kecil**	[dʒalan ketʃil]
park	**taman**	[taman]
boulevard	**bulevar, adimarga**	[bulevar], [adimarga]
square	**lapangan**	[lapaŋan]
avenue (wide street)	**jalan raya**	[dʒalan raja]
street	**jalan**	[dʒalan]
side street	**gang**	[gaŋ]
dead end	**jalan buntu**	[dʒalan buntu]
house	**rumah**	[rumah]
building	**gedung**	[geduŋ]
skyscraper	**pencakar langit**	[pentʃakar laŋit]
facade	**bagian depan**	[bagian depan]
roof	**atap**	[atap]
window	**jendela**	[dʒendela]
arch	**lengkungan**	[leŋkuŋan]
column	**pilar**	[pilar]
corner	**sudut**	[sudut]
shop window	**etalase**	[etalase]
signboard (store sign, etc.)	**papan nama**	[papan nama]
poster (e.g., playbill)	**poster**	[poster]

advertising poster	**poster iklan**	[poster iklan]
hoarding	**papan iklan**	[papan iklan]
rubbish	**sampah**	[sampah]
rubbish bin	**tong sampah**	[toŋ sampah]
to litter (vi)	**menyampah**	[mənjampah]
rubbish dump	**tempat pemrosesan akhir (TPA)**	[tempat pemrosesan ahir]
telephone box	**gardu telepon umum**	[gardu telepon umum]
lamppost	**tiang lampu**	[tiaŋ lampu]
bench (park ~)	**bangku**	[baŋku]
police officer	**polisi**	[polisi]
police	**polisi, kepolisian**	[polisi], [kepolisian]
beggar	**pengemis**	[peŋemis]
homeless (n)	**tuna wisma**	[tuna wisma]

29. Urban institutions

shop	**toko**	[toko]
chemist, pharmacy	**apotek, toko obat**	[apotek], [toko obat]
optician (spectacles shop)	**optik**	[opti']
shopping centre	**toserba**	[toserba]
supermarket	**pasar swalayan**	[pasar swalajan]
bakery	**toko roti**	[toko roti]
baker	**pembuat roti**	[pembuat roti]
cake shop	**toko kue**	[toko kue]
grocery shop	**toko pangan**	[toko paŋan]
butcher shop	**toko daging**	[toko dagiŋ]
greengrocer	**toko sayur**	[toko sajur]
market	**pasar**	[pasar]
coffee bar	**warung kopi**	[waruŋ kopi]
restaurant	**restoran**	[restoran]
pub, bar	**kedai bir**	[kedaj bir]
pizzeria	**kedai piza**	[kedaj piza]
hairdresser	**salon rambut**	[salon rambut]
post office	**kantor pos**	[kantor pos]
dry cleaners	**penatu kimia**	[penatu kimia]
photo studio	**studio foto**	[studio foto]
shoe shop	**toko sepatu**	[toko sepatu]
bookshop	**toko buku**	[toko buku]
sports shop	**toko alat olahraga**	[toko alat olahraga]
clothes repair shop	**reparasi pakaian**	[reparasi pakajan]
formal wear hire	**rental pakaian**	[rental pakajan]
video rental shop	**rental film**	[rental film]
circus	**sirkus**	[sirkus]
zoo	**kebun binatang**	[kebun binataŋ]

cinema	**bioskop**	[bioskop]
museum	**museum**	[museum]
library	**perpustakaan**	[pərpustaka'an]
theatre	**teater**	[teater]
opera (opera house)	**opera**	[opera]
nightclub	**klub malam**	[klub malam]
casino	**kasino**	[kasino]
mosque	**masjid**	[masdʒid]
synagogue	**sinagoga, kanisah**	[sinagoga], [kanisah]
cathedral	**katedral**	[katedral]
temple	**kuil, candi**	[kuil], [tʃandi]
church	**gereja**	[geredʒa]
college	**institut, perguruan tinggi**	[institut], [pərguruan tiŋgi]
university	**universitas**	[universitas]
school	**sekolah**	[sekolah]
prefecture	**prefektur, distrik**	[prefektur], [distri']
town hall	**balai kota**	[balaj kota]
hotel	**hotel**	[hotel]
bank	**bank**	[ban']
embassy	**kedutaan besar**	[keduta'an besar]
travel agency	**kantor pariwisata**	[kantor pariwisata]
information office	**kantor penerangan**	[kantor peneraŋan]
currency exchange	**kantor penukaran uang**	[kantor penukaran uaŋ]
underground, tube	**kereta api bawah tanah**	[kereta api bawah tanah]
hospital	**rumah sakit**	[rumah sakit]
petrol station	**SPBU, stasiun bensin**	[es-pe-be-u], [stasjun bensin]
car park	**tempat parkir**	[tempat parkir]

30. Signs

signboard (store sign, etc.)	**papan nama**	[papan nama]
notice (door sign, etc.)	**tulisan**	[tulisan]
poster	**poster**	[poster]
direction sign	**penunjuk arah**	[penundʒu' arah]
arrow (sign)	**anak panah**	[ana' panah]
caution	**peringatan**	[periŋatan]
warning sign	**tanda peringatan**	[tanda periŋatan]
to warn (vt)	**memperingatkan**	[memperiŋatkan]
rest day (weekly ~)	**hari libur**	[hari libur]
timetable (schedule)	**jadwal**	[dʒadwal]
opening hours	**jam buka**	[dʒam buka]
WELCOME!	**SELAMAT DATANG!**	[selamat dataŋ!]
ENTRANCE	**MASUK**	[masu']
WAY OUT	**KELUAR**	[keluar]

PUSH	DORONG	[doroŋ]
PULL	TARIK	[tariʔ]
OPEN	BUKA	[buka]
CLOSED	TUTUP	[tutup]

| WOMEN | WANITA | [wanita] |
| MEN | PRIA | [pria] |

DISCOUNTS	DISKON	[diskon]
SALE	OBRAL	[obral]
NEW!	BARU!	[baru!]
FREE	GRATIS	[gratis]

ATTENTION!	PERHATIAN!	[pərhatian!]
NO VACANCIES	PENUH	[penuh]
RESERVED	DIRESERVASI	[direservasi]

| ADMINISTRATION | ADMINISTRASI | [administrasi] |
| STAFF ONLY | KHUSUS STAF | [husus staf] |

BEWARE OF THE DOG!	AWAS, ANJING GALAK!	[awas], [andʒiŋ galaʔ!]
NO SMOKING	DILARANG MEROKOK!	[dilaraŋ merokoʔ!]
DO NOT TOUCH!	JANGAN SENTUH!	[dʒaŋan sentuh!]

DANGEROUS	BERBAHAYA	[berbahaja]
DANGER	BAHAYA	[bahaja]
HIGH VOLTAGE	TEGANGAN TINGGI	[tegaŋan tiŋgi]
NO SWIMMING!	DILARANG BERENANG!	[dilaraŋ berenaŋ!]
OUT OF ORDER	RUSAK	[rusaʔ]

FLAMMABLE	BAHAN MUDAH TERBAKAR	[bahan mudah terbakar]
FORBIDDEN	DILARANG	[dilaraŋ]
NO TRESPASSING!	DILARANG MASUK!	[dilaraŋ masuʔ!]
WET PAINT	AWAS CAT BASAH	[awas tʃat basah]

31. Shopping

to buy (purchase)	membeli	[membeli]
shopping	belanjaan	[belandʒaʔaʔan]
to go shopping	berbelanja	[berbelandʒa]
shopping	berbelanja	[berbelandʒa]

| to be open (ab. shop) | buka | [buka] |
| to be closed | tutup | [tutup] |

footwear, shoes	sepatu	[sepatu]
clothes, clothing	pakaian	[pakajan]
cosmetics	kosmetik	[kosmetiʔ]
food products	produk makanan	[produʔ makanan]
gift, present	hadiah	[hadiah]

| shop assistant (masc.) | pramuniaga | [pramuniaga] |
| shop assistant (fem.) | pramuniaga perempuan | [pramuniaga perempuan] |

cash desk	**kas**	[kas]
mirror	**cermin**	[ʧermin]
counter (shop ~)	**konter**	[konter]
fitting room	**kamar pas**	[kamar pas]
to try on	**mengepas**	[məŋepas]
to fit (ab. dress, etc.)	**pas, cocok**	[pas], [ʧoʧoʔ]
to fancy (vt)	**suka**	[suka]
price	**harga**	[harga]
price tag	**label harga**	[label harga]
to cost (vt)	**berharga**	[bərharga]
How much?	**Berapa?**	[bərapa?]
discount	**diskon**	[diskon]
inexpensive (adj)	**tidak mahal**	[tidaʔ mahal]
cheap (adj)	**murah**	[murah]
expensive (adj)	**mahal**	[mahal]
It's expensive	**Ini mahal**	[ini mahal]
hire (n)	**rental, persewaan**	[rental], [pərsewa'an]
to hire (~ a dinner jacket)	**menyewa**	[mənjewa]
credit (trade credit)	**kredit**	[kredit]
on credit (adv)	**secara kredit**	[seʧara kredit]

CLOTHING & ACCESSORIES

32. Outerwear. Coats

clothes	pakaian	[pakajan]
outerwear	pakaian luar	[pakajan luar]
winter clothing	pakaian musim dingin	[pakajan musim diŋin]
coat (overcoat)	mantel	[mantel]
fur coat	mantel bulu	[mantel bulu]
fur jacket	jaket bulu	[dʒʲaket bulu]
down coat	jaket bulu halus	[dʒʲaket bulu halus]
jacket (e.g. leather ~)	jaket	[dʒʲaket]
raincoat (trenchcoat, etc.)	jas hujan	[dʒʲas hudʒʲan]
waterproof (adj)	kedap air	[kedap air]

33. Men's & women's clothing

shirt (button shirt)	kemeja	[kemedʒʲa]
trousers	celana	[tʃelana]
jeans	celana jins	[tʃelana dʒins]
suit jacket	jas	[dʒʲas]
suit	setelan	[setelan]
dress (frock)	gaun	[gaun]
skirt	rok	[roʔ]
blouse	blus	[blus]
knitted jacket (cardigan, etc.)	jaket wol	[dʒʲaket wol]
jacket (of a woman's suit)	jaket	[dʒʲaket]
T-shirt	baju kaus	[badʒʲu kaus]
shorts (short trousers)	celana pendek	[tʃelana pendeʔ]
tracksuit	pakaian olahraga	[pakajan olahraga]
bathrobe	jubah mandi	[dʒʲubah mandi]
pyjamas	piyama	[piyama]
jumper (sweater)	sweter	[sweter]
pullover	pulover	[pulover]
waistcoat	rompi	[rompi]
tailcoat	jas berbuntut	[dʒʲas berbuntut]
dinner suit	jas malam	[dʒʲas malam]
uniform	seragam	[seragam]
workwear	pakaian kerja	[pakajan kerdʒʲa]
boiler suit	baju monyet	[badʒʲu monjet]
coat (e.g. doctor's smock)	jas	[dʒʲas]

34. Clothing. Underwear

underwear	**pakaian dalam**	[pakajan dalam]
pants	**celana dalam lelaki**	[tɕelana dalam lelaki]
panties	**celana dalam wanita**	[tɕelana dalam wanita]
vest (singlet)	**singlet**	[siŋlet]
socks	**kaus kaki**	[kaus kaki]
nightdress	**baju tidur**	[badʒʲu tidur]
bra	**beha**	[beha]
knee highs (knee-high socks)	**kaus kaki selutut**	[kaus kaki selutut]
tights	**pantihos**	[pantihos]
stockings (hold ups)	**kaus kaki panjang**	[kaus kaki pandʒʲaŋ]
swimsuit, bikini	**baju renang**	[badʒʲu renaŋ]

35. Headwear

hat	**topi**	[topi]
trilby hat	**topi bulat**	[topi bulat]
baseball cap	**topi bisbol**	[topi bisbol]
flatcap	**topi pet**	[topi pet]
beret	**baret**	[baret]
hood	**kerudung kepala**	[keruduŋ kepala]
panama hat	**topi panama**	[topi panama]
knit cap (knitted hat)	**topi rajut**	[topi radʒʲut]
headscarf	**tudung kepala**	[tuduŋ kepala]
women's hat	**topi wanita**	[topi wanita]
hard hat	**topi baja**	[topi badʒʲa]
forage cap	**topi lipat**	[topi lipat]
helmet	**helm**	[helm]
bowler	**topi bulat**	[topi bulat]
top hat	**topi tinggi**	[topi tiŋgi]

36. Footwear

footwear	**sepatu**	[sepatu]
shoes (men's shoes)	**sepatu bot**	[sepatu bot]
shoes (women's shoes)	**sepatu wanita**	[sepatu wanita]
boots (e.g., cowboy ~)	**sepatu lars**	[sepatu lars]
carpet slippers	**pantofel**	[pantofel]
trainers	**sepatu tenis**	[sepatu tenis]
trainers	**sepatu kets**	[sepatu kets]
sandals	**sandal**	[sandal]
cobbler (shoe repairer)	**tukang sepatu**	[tukaŋ sepatu]
heel	**tumit**	[tumit]

pair (of shoes)	sepasang	[sepasaŋ]
lace (shoelace)	tali sepatu	[tali sepatu]
to lace up (vt)	mengikat tali	[məŋikat tali]
shoehorn	sendok sepatu	[sendo' sepatu]
shoe polish	semir sepatu	[semir sepatu]

37. Personal accessories

gloves	sarung tangan	[saruŋ taŋan]
mittens	sarung tangan	[saruŋ taŋan]
scarf (muffler)	selendang	[selendaŋ]

glasses	kacamata	[katʃamata]
frame (eyeglass ~)	bingkai	[biŋkaj]
umbrella	payung	[pajuŋ]
walking stick	tongkat jalan	[toŋkat dʒ¡alan]
hairbrush	sikat rambut	[sikat rambut]
fan	kipas	[kipas]

tie (necktie)	dasi	[dasi]
bow tie	dasi kupu-kupu	[dasi kupu-kupu]
braces	bretel	[bretel]
handkerchief	sapu tangan	[sapu taŋan]

comb	sisir	[sisir]
hair slide	jepit rambut	[dʒ¡epit rambut]
hairpin	harnal	[harnal]
buckle	gesper	[gesper]

| belt | sabuk | [sabu'] |
| shoulder strap | tali tas | [tali tas] |

bag (handbag)	tas	[tas]
handbag	tas tangan	[tas taŋan]
rucksack	ransel	[ransel]

38. Clothing. Miscellaneous

fashion	mode	[mode]
in vogue (adj)	modis	[modis]
fashion designer	perancang busana	[pərantʃaŋ busana]

collar	kerah	[kerah]
pocket	saku	[saku]
pocket (as adj)	saku	[saku]
sleeve	lengan	[leŋan]
hanging loop	tali kait	[tali kait]
flies (on trousers)	golbi	[golbi]

zip (fastener)	ritsleting	[ritsletiŋ]
fastener	kancing	[kantʃiŋ]
button	kancing	[kantʃiŋ]

| buttonhole | lubang kancing | [lubaŋ kantʃiŋ] |
| to come off (ab. button) | terlepas | [tərlepas] |

to sew (vi, vt)	menjahit	[məndʒ'ahit]
to embroider (vi, vt)	membordir	[membordir]
embroidery	bordiran	[bordiran]
sewing needle	jarum	[dʒ'arum]
thread	benang	[benaŋ]
seam	setik	[seti']

to get dirty (vi)	kena kotor	[kena kotor]
stain (mark, spot)	bercak	[bertʃa']
to crease, to crumple	kumal	[kumal]
to tear, to rip (vt)	merobek	[merobe']
clothes moth	ngengat	[ŋeŋat]

39. Personal care. Cosmetics

toothpaste	pasta gigi	[pasta gigi]
toothbrush	sikat gigi	[sikat gigi]
to clean one's teeth	menggosok gigi	[məŋgoso' gigi]

razor	pisau cukur	[pisau tʃukur]
shaving cream	krim cukur	[krim tʃukur]
to shave (vi)	bercukur	[bərtʃukur]

| soap | sabun | [sabun] |
| shampoo | sampo | [sampo] |

scissors	gunting	[guntiŋ]
nail file	kikir kuku	[kikir kuku]
nail clippers	pemotong kuku	[pemotoŋ kuku]
tweezers	pinset	[pinset]

cosmetics	kosmetik	[kosmeti']
face mask	masker	[masker]
manicure	manikur	[manikur]
to have a manicure	melakukan manikur	[melakukan manikur]
pedicure	pedi	[pedi]

make-up bag	tas kosmetik	[tas kosmeti']
face powder	bedak	[beda']
powder compact	kotak bedak	[kota' beda']
blusher	perona pipi	[pərona pipi]

perfume (bottled)	parfum	[parfum]
toilet water (lotion)	minyak wangi	[minja' waŋi]
lotion	losion	[losjon]
cologne	kolonye	[kolone]

eyeshadow	pewarna mata	[pewarna mata]
eyeliner	pensil alis	[pensil alis]
mascara	celak	[tʃela']
lipstick	lipstik	[lipsti']

nail polish	**kuteks, cat kuku**	[kuteks], [tʃat kuku]
hair spray	**semprotan rambut**	[semprotan rambut]
deodorant	**deodoran**	[deodoran]

cream	**krim**	[krim]
face cream	**krim wajah**	[krim wadʒʲah]
hand cream	**krim tangan**	[krim taŋan]
anti-wrinkle cream	**krim antikerut**	[krim antikerut]
day cream	**krim siang**	[krim siaŋ]
night cream	**krim malam**	[krim malam]
day (as adj)	**siang**	[siaŋ]
night (as adj)	**malam**	[malam]

tampon	**tampon**	[tampon]
toilet paper (toilet roll)	**kertas toilet**	[kertas toylet]
hair dryer	**pengering rambut**	[peŋeriŋ rambut]

40. Watches. Clocks

watch (wristwatch)	**arloji**	[arlodʒi]
dial	**piringan jam**	[piriŋan dʒʲam]
hand (clock, watch)	**jarum**	[dʒʲarum]
metal bracelet	**rantai arloji**	[rantaj arlodʒi]
watch strap	**tali arloji**	[tali arlodʒi]

battery	**baterai**	[bateraj]
to be flat (battery)	**mati**	[mati]
to change a battery	**mengganti baterai**	[meŋganti bateraj]
to run fast	**cepat**	[tʃepat]
to run slow	**terlambat**	[terlambat]

wall clock	**jam dinding**	[dʒʲam dindiŋ]
hourglass	**jam pasir**	[dʒʲam pasir]
sundial	**jam matahari**	[dʒʲam matahari]
alarm clock	**weker**	[weker]
watchmaker	**tukang jam**	[tukaŋ dʒʲam]
to repair (vt)	**mereparasi, memperbaiki**	[mereparasi], [memperbajki]

EVERYDAY EXPERIENCE

41. Money

money	**uang**	[uaŋ]
currency exchange	**pertukaran mata uang**	[pərtukaran mata uaŋ]
exchange rate	**nilai tukar**	[nilaj tukar]
cashpoint	**Anjungan Tunai Mandiri, ATM**	[andʒuŋan tunaj mandiri], [a-te-em]
coin	**koin**	[koin]
dollar	**dolar**	[dolar]
euro	**euro**	[euro]
lira	**lira**	[lira]
Deutschmark	**Mark Jerman**	[marˀ dʒˈerman]
franc	**franc**	[frantʃ]
pound sterling	**poundsterling**	[paundsterliŋ]
yen	**yen**	[yen]
debt	**utang**	[utaŋ]
debtor	**pengutang**	[pəŋutaŋ]
to lend (money)	**meminjamkan**	[memindʒˈamkan]
to borrow (vi, vt)	**meminjam**	[memindʒˈam]
bank	**bank**	[banˀ]
account	**rekening**	[rekeniŋ]
to deposit (vt)	**memasukkan**	[memasuˀkan]
to deposit into the account	**memasukkan ke rekening**	[memasuˀkan ke rekeniŋ]
to withdraw (vt)	**menarik uang**	[mənariˀ uaŋ]
credit card	**kartu kredit**	[kartu kredit]
cash	**uang kontan, uang tunai**	[uaŋ kontan], [uaŋ tunaj]
cheque	**cek**	[tʃeˀ]
to write a cheque	**menulis cek**	[mənulis tʃeˀ]
chequebook	**buku cek**	[buku tʃeˀ]
wallet	**dompet**	[dompet]
purse	**dompet, pundi-pundi**	[dompet], [pundi-pundi]
safe	**brankas**	[brankas]
heir	**pewaris**	[pewaris]
inheritance	**warisan**	[warisan]
fortune (wealth)	**kekayaan**	[kekajaˀan]
lease	**sewa**	[sewa]
rent (money)	**uang sewa**	[uaŋ sewa]
to rent (sth from sb)	**menyewa**	[mənjewa]
price	**harga**	[harga]
cost	**harga**	[harga]

sum	jumlah	[dʒjumlah]
to spend (vt)	menghabiskan	[məŋhabiskan]
expenses	ongkos	[oŋkos]
to economize (vi, vt)	menghemat	[məŋhemat]
economical	hemat	[hemat]

to pay (vi, vt)	membayar	[membajar]
payment	pembayaran	[pembajaran]
change (give the ~)	kembalian	[kembalian]

tax	pajak	[padʒja']
fine	denda	[denda]
to fine (vt)	mendenda	[məndenda]

42. Post. Postal service

post office	kantor pos	[kantor pos]
post (letters, etc.)	surat	[surat]
postman	tukang pos	[tukaŋ pos]
opening hours	jam buka	[dʒjam buka]

letter	surat	[surat]
registered letter	surat tercatat	[surat tərtʃatat]
postcard	kartu pos	[kartu pos]
telegram	telegram	[telegram]
parcel	parsel, paket pos	[parsel], [paket pos]
money transfer	wesel pos	[wesel pos]

to receive (vt)	menerima	[mənerima]
to send (vt)	mengirim	[məŋirim]
sending	pengiriman	[peŋiriman]
address	alamat	[alamat]
postcode	kode pos	[kode pos]
sender	pengirim	[peŋirim]
receiver	penerima	[penerima]

name (first name)	nama	[nama]
surname (last name)	nama keluarga	[nama keluarga]
postage rate	tarif	[tarif]
standard (adj)	biasa, standar	[biasa], [standar]
economical (adj)	ekonomis	[ekonomis]

weight	berat	[berat]
to weigh (~ letters)	menimbang	[mənimbaŋ]
envelope	amplop	[amplop]
postage stamp	prangko	[praŋko]
to stamp an envelope	menempelkan prangko	[mənempelkan praŋko]

43. Banking

| bank | bank | [ban'] |
| branch (of a bank) | cabang | [tʃabaŋ] |

| consultant | konsultan | [konsultan] |
| manager (director) | manajer | [manadʒer] |

bank account	rekening	[rekeniŋ]
account number	nomor rekening	[nomor rekeniŋ]
current account	rekening koran	[rekeniŋ koran]
deposit account	rekening simpanan	[rekeniŋ simpanan]

to open an account	membuka rekening	[membuka rekeniŋ]
to close the account	menutup rekening	[mənutup rekeniŋ]
to deposit into the account	memasukkan ke rekening	[memasuʔkan ke rekeniŋ]
to withdraw (vt)	menarik uang	[mənariʔ uaŋ]

deposit	deposito	[deposito]
to make a deposit	melakukan setoran	[melakukan setoran]
wire transfer	transfer kawat	[transfer kawat]
to wire, to transfer	mentransfer	[mentransfer]

| sum | jumlah | [dʒumlah] |
| How much? | Berapa? | [berapa?] |

| signature | tanda tangan | [tanda taŋan] |
| to sign (vt) | menandatangani | [mənandataŋani] |

credit card	kartu kredit	[kartu kredit]
code (PIN code)	kode	[kode]
credit card number	nomor kartu kredit	[nomor kartu kredit]
cashpoint	Anjungan Tunai Mandiri, ATM	[andʒuŋan tunaj mandiri], [a-te-em]

cheque	cek	[tʃeʔ]
to write a cheque	menulis cek	[mənulis tʃeʔ]
chequebook	buku cek	[buku tʃeʔ]

loan (bank ~)	kredit, pinjaman	[kredit], [pindʒaman]
to apply for a loan	meminta kredit	[meminta kredit]
to get a loan	mendapatkan kredit	[məndapatkan kredit]
to give a loan	memberikan kredit	[memberikan kredit]
guarantee	jaminan	[dʒaminan]

44. Telephone. Phone conversation

telephone	telepon	[telepon]
mobile phone	ponsel	[ponsel]
answerphone	mesin penjawab panggilan	[mesin pendʒawab paŋgilan]

| to call (by phone) | menelepon | [menelepon] |
| call, ring | panggilan telepon | [paŋgilan telepon] |

to dial a number	memutar nomor telepon	[memutar nomor telepon]
Hello!	Halo!	[halo!]
to ask (vt)	bertanya	[bertanja]
to answer (vi, vt)	menjawab	[mendʒawab]
to hear (vt)	mendengar	[mendeŋar]

well (adv)	baik	[baj']
not well (adv)	buruk, jelek	[buruk], [dʒˈele']
noises (interference)	bising, gangguan	[bisiŋ], [gaŋguan]
receiver	gagang	[gagaŋ]
to pick up (~ the phone)	mengangkat telepon	[məŋaŋkat telepon]
to hang up (~ the phone)	menutup telepon	[mənutup telepon]
busy (engaged)	sibuk	[sibu']
to ring (ab. phone)	berdering	[bərderiŋ]
telephone book	buku telepon	[buku telepon]
local (adj)	lokal	[lokal]
local call	panggilan lokal	[paŋgilan lokal]
trunk (e.g. ~ call)	interlokal	[interlokal]
trunk call	panggilan interlokal	[paŋgilan interlokal]
international (adj)	internasional	[internasional]
international call	panggilan internasional	[paŋgilan internasional]

45. Mobile telephone

mobile phone	ponsel	[ponsel]
display	layar	[lajar]
button	kenop	[kenop]
SIM card	kartu SIM	[kartu sim]
battery	baterai	[bateraj]
to be flat (battery)	mati	[mati]
charger	pengisi baterai, pengecas	[pəŋisi bateraj], [pəŋetʃas]
menu	menu	[menu]
settings	penyetelan	[penjetelan]
tune (melody)	nada panggil	[nada paŋgil]
to select (vt)	memilih	[memilih]
calculator	kalkulator	[kalkulator]
voice mail	penjawab telepon	[pendʒˈawab telepon]
alarm clock	weker	[weker]
contacts	buku telepon	[buku telepon]
SMS (text message)	pesan singkat	[pesan siŋkat]
subscriber	pelanggan	[pelaŋgan]

46. Stationery

ballpoint pen	bolpen	[bolpen]
fountain pen	pena celup	[pena tʃelup]
pencil	pensil	[pensil]
highlighter	spidol	[spidol]
felt-tip pen	spidol	[spidol]
notepad	buku catatan	[buku tʃatatan]

diary	agenda	[agenda]
ruler	mistar, penggaris	[mistar], [penggaris]
calculator	kalkulator	[kalkulator]
rubber	karet penghapus	[karet penhapus]
drawing pin	paku payung	[paku pajuŋ]
paper clip	penjepit kertas	[pendʒiepit kertas]
glue	lem	[lem]
stapler	stapler	[stapler]
hole punch	alat pelubang kertas	[alat pelubaŋ kertas]
pencil sharpener	rautan pensil	[rautan pensil]

47. Foreign languages

language	bahasa	[bahasa]
foreign (adj)	asing	[asiŋ]
foreign language	bahasa asing	[bahasa asiŋ]
to study (vt)	mempelajari	[mempeladʒiari]
to learn (language, etc.)	belajar	[beladʒiar]
to read (vi, vt)	membaca	[membatʃa]
to speak (vi, vt)	berbicara	[berbitʃara]
to understand (vt)	mengerti	[meŋerti]
to write (vt)	menulis	[menulis]
fast (adv)	cepat, fasih	[tʃepat], [fasih]
slowly (adv)	perlahan-lahan	[perlahan-lahan]
fluently (adv)	fasih	[fasih]
rules	peraturan	[peraturan]
grammar	tatabahasa	[tatabahasa]
vocabulary	kosakata	[kosakata]
phonetics	fonetik	[foneti?]
textbook	buku pelajaran	[buku peladʒiaran]
dictionary	kamus	[kamus]
teach-yourself book	buku autodidak	[buku autodida?]
phrasebook	panduan percakapan	[panduan pertʃakapan]
cassette, tape	kaset	[kaset]
videotape	kaset video	[kaset video]
CD, compact disc	cakram kompak	[tʃakram kompa?]
DVD	cakram DVD	[tʃakram di-vi-di]
alphabet	alfabet, abjad	[alfabet], [abdʒiad]
to spell (vt)	mengeja	[meŋedʒia]
pronunciation	pelafalan	[pelafalan]
accent	aksen	[aksen]
with an accent	dengan aksen	[deŋan aksen]
without an accent	tanpa aksen	[tanpa aksen]
word	kata	[kata]
meaning	arti	[arti]

course (e.g. a French ~)	**kursus**	[kursus]
to sign up	**Mendaftar**	[məndaftar]
teacher	**guru**	[guru]
translation (process)	**penerjemahan**	[penerdʒʲemahan]
translation (text, etc.)	**terjemahan**	[tərdʒʲemahan]
translator	**penerjemah**	[penerdʒʲemah]
interpreter	**juru bahasa**	[dʒʲuru bahasa]
polyglot	**poliglot**	[poliglot]
memory	**memori, daya ingat**	[memori], [daja iŋat]

MEALS. RESTAURANT

48. Table setting

spoon	sendok	[sendo']
knife	pisau	[pisau]
fork	garpu	[garpu]
cup (e.g., coffee ~)	cangkir	[tʃaŋkir]
plate (dinner ~)	piring	[piriŋ]
saucer	alas cangkir	[alas tʃaŋkir]
serviette	serbet	[serbet]
toothpick	tusuk gigi	[tusu' gigi]

49. Restaurant

restaurant	restoran	[restoran]
coffee bar	warung kopi	[waruŋ kopi]
pub, bar	bar	[bar]
tearoom	warung teh	[waruŋ teh]
waiter	pelayan lelaki	[pelajan lelaki]
waitress	pelayan perempuan	[pelajan perempuan]
barman	pelayan bar	[pelajan bar]
menu	menu	[menu]
wine list	daftar anggur	[daftar aŋgur]
to book a table	memesan meja	[memesan medʒ'a]
course, dish	masakan, hidangan	[masakan], [hidaŋan]
to order (meal)	memesan	[memesan]
to make an order	memesan	[memesan]
aperitif	aperitif	[aperitif]
starter	makanan ringan	[makanan riŋan]
dessert, pudding	hidangan penutup	[hidaŋan penutup]
bill	bon	[bon]
to pay the bill	membayar bon	[membajar bon]
to give change	memberikan uang kembalian	[memberikan uaŋ kembalian]
tip	tip	[tip]

50. Meals

| food | makanan | [makanan] |
| to eat (vi, vt) | makan | [makan] |

breakfast	makan pagi, sarapan	[makan pagi], [sarapan]
to have breakfast	sarapan	[sarapan]
lunch	makan siang	[makan siaŋ]
to have lunch	makan siang	[makan siaŋ]
dinner	makan malam	[makan malam]
to have dinner	makan malam	[makan malam]
appetite	nafsu makan	[nafsu makan]
Enjoy your meal!	Selamat makan!	[selamat makan!]
to open (~ a bottle)	membuka	[membuka]
to spill (liquid)	menumpahkan	[mənumpahkan]
to boil (vi)	mendidih	[məndidih]
to boil (vt)	mendidihkan	[məndidihkan]
boiled (~ water)	masak	[masaʔ]
to chill, cool down (vt)	mendinginkan	[məndiŋinkan]
to chill (vi)	mendingin	[məndiŋin]
taste, flavour	rasa	[rasa]
aftertaste	nuansa rasa	[nuansa rasa]
to slim down (lose weight)	berdiet	[berdiet]
diet	diet, pola makan	[diet], [pola makan]
vitamin	vitamin	[vitamin]
calorie	kalori	[kalori]
vegetarian (n)	vegetarian	[vegetarian]
vegetarian (adj)	vegetarian	[vegetarian]
fats (nutrient)	lemak	[lemaʔ]
proteins	protein	[protein]
carbohydrates	karbohidrat	[karbohidrat]
slice (of lemon, ham)	irisan	[irisan]
piece (of cake, pie)	potongan	[potoŋan]
crumb (of bread, cake, etc.)	remah	[remah]

51. Cooked dishes

course, dish	masakan, hidangan	[masakan], [hidaŋan]
cuisine	masakan	[masakan]
recipe	resep	[resep]
portion	porsi	[porsi]
salad	salada	[salada]
soup	sup	[sup]
clear soup (broth)	kaldu	[kaldu]
sandwich (bread)	roti lapis	[roti lapis]
fried eggs	telur mata sapi	[telur mata sapi]
hamburger (beefburger)	hamburger	[hamburger]
beefsteak	bistik	[bistiʔ]
side dish	lauk	[lauʔ]

spaghetti	**spageti**	[spageti]
mash	**kentang tumbuk**	[kentaŋ tumbuʔ]
pizza	**piza**	[piza]
porridge (oatmeal, etc.)	**bubur**	[bubur]
omelette	**telur dadar**	[telur dadar]
boiled (e.g. ~ beef)	**rebus**	[rebus]
smoked (adj)	**asap**	[asap]
fried (adj)	**goreng**	[goreŋ]
dried (adj)	**kering**	[keriŋ]
frozen (adj)	**beku**	[beku]
pickled (adj)	**marinade**	[marinade]
sweet (sugary)	**manis**	[manis]
salty (adj)	**asin**	[asin]
cold (adj)	**dingin**	[diŋin]
hot (adj)	**panas**	[panas]
bitter (adj)	**pahit**	[pahit]
tasty (adj)	**enak**	[enaʔ]
to cook in boiling water	**merebus**	[merebus]
to cook (dinner)	**memasak**	[memasaʔ]
to fry (vt)	**menggoreng**	[məŋgoreŋ]
to heat up (food)	**memanaskan**	[memanaskan]
to salt (vt)	**menggarami**	[məŋgarami]
to pepper (vt)	**membubuh merica**	[membubuh meritʃa]
to grate (vt)	**memarut**	[memarut]
peel (n)	**kulit**	[kulit]
to peel (vt)	**mengupas**	[məŋupas]

52. Food

meat	**daging**	[dagiŋ]
chicken	**ayam**	[ajam]
poussin	**anak ayam**	[anaʼ ajam]
duck	**bebek**	[bebeʔ]
goose	**angsa**	[aŋsa]
game	**binatang buruan**	[binataŋ buruan]
turkey	**kalkun**	[kalkun]
pork	**daging babi**	[dagiŋ babi]
veal	**daging anak sapi**	[dagiŋ anaʼ sapi]
lamb	**daging domba**	[dagiŋ domba]
beef	**daging sapi**	[dagiŋ sapi]
rabbit	**kelinci**	[kelintʃi]
sausage (bologna, etc.)	**sosis**	[sosis]
vienna sausage (frankfurter)	**sosis**	[sosis]
bacon	**bakon**	[beykon]
ham	**ham, daging kornet**	[ham], [dagiŋ kornet]
gammon	**ham**	[ham]
pâté	**pasta**	[pasta]
liver	**hati**	[hati]

mince (minced meat)	**daging giling**	[dagiŋ giliŋ]
tongue	**lidah**	[lidah]
egg	**telur**	[telur]
eggs	**telur**	[telur]
egg white	**putih telur**	[putih telur]
egg yolk	**kuning telur**	[kuniŋ telur]
fish	**ikan**	[ikan]
seafood	**makanan laut**	[makanan laut]
crustaceans	**krustasea**	[krustasea]
caviar	**caviar**	[kaviar]
crab	**kepiting**	[kepitiŋ]
prawn	**udang**	[udaŋ]
oyster	**tiram**	[tiram]
spiny lobster	**lobster berduri**	[lobster bərduri]
octopus	**gurita**	[gurita]
squid	**cumi-cumi**	[ʧumi-ʧumi]
sturgeon	**ikan sturgeon**	[ikan sturdʒ'en]
salmon	**salmon**	[salmon]
halibut	**ikan turbot**	[ikan turbot]
cod	**ikan kod**	[ikan kod]
mackerel	**ikan kembung**	[ikan kembuŋ]
tuna	**tuna**	[tuna]
eel	**belut**	[belut]
trout	**ikan forel**	[ikan forel]
sardine	**sarden**	[sarden]
pike	**ikan pike**	[ikan paik]
herring	**ikan haring**	[ikan hariŋ]
bread	**roti**	[roti]
cheese	**keju**	[kedʒ'u]
sugar	**gula**	[gula]
salt	**garam**	[garam]
rice	**beras, nasi**	[beras], [nasi]
pasta (macaroni)	**makaroni**	[makaroni]
noodles	**mi**	[mi]
butter	**mentega**	[məntega]
vegetable oil	**minyak nabati**	[minja' nabati]
sunflower oil	**minyak bunga matahari**	[minja' buŋa matahari]
margarine	**margarin**	[margarin]
olives	**buah zaitun**	[buah zajtun]
olive oil	**minyak zaitun**	[minja' zajtun]
milk	**susu**	[susu]
condensed milk	**susu kental**	[susu kental]
yogurt	**yogurt**	[yogurt]
soured cream	**krim asam**	[krim asam]
cream (of milk)	**krim, kepala susu**	[krim], [kepala susu]

mayonnaise	**mayones**	[majones]
buttercream	**krim**	[krim]
groats (barley ~, etc.)	**menir**	[menir]
flour	**tepung**	[tepuŋ]
tinned food	**makanan kalengan**	[makanan kaleŋan]
cornflakes	**emping jagung**	[empiŋ dʒⁱaguŋ]
honey	**madu**	[madu]
jam	**selai**	[selaj]
chewing gum	**permen karet**	[permen karet]

53. Drinks

water	**air**	[air]
drinking water	**air minum**	[air minum]
mineral water	**air mineral**	[air mineral]
still (adj)	**tanpa gas**	[tanpa gas]
carbonated (adj)	**berkarbonasi**	[berkarbonasi]
sparkling (adj)	**bergas**	[bergas]
ice	**es**	[es]
with ice	**dengan es**	[deŋan es]
non-alcoholic (adj)	**tanpa alkohol**	[tanpa alkohol]
soft drink	**minuman ringan**	[minuman riŋan]
refreshing drink	**minuman penygar**	[minuman penigar]
lemonade	**limun**	[limun]
spirits	**minoman beralkohol**	[minoman beralkohol]
wine	**anggur**	[aŋgur]
white wine	**anggur putih**	[aŋgur putih]
red wine	**anggur merah**	[aŋgur merah]
liqueur	**likeur**	[likeur]
champagne	**sampanye**	[sampanje]
vermouth	**vermouth**	[vermut]
whisky	**wiski**	[wiski]
vodka	**vodka**	[vodka]
gin	**jin, jenewer**	[dʒin], [dʒⁱenewer]
cognac	**konyak**	[konjaʔ]
rum	**rum**	[rum]
coffee	**kopi**	[kopi]
black coffee	**kopi pahit**	[kopi pahit]
white coffee	**kopi susu**	[kopi susu]
cappuccino	**cappuccino**	[kaputʃino]
instant coffee	**kopi instan**	[kopi instan]
milk	**susu**	[susu]
cocktail	**koktail**	[koktajl]
milkshake	**susu kocok**	[susu kotʃoʔ]
juice	**jus**	[dʒⁱus]

tomato juice	**jus tomat**	[dʒʲus tomat]
orange juice	**jus jeruk**	[dʒʲus dʒʲeruʔ]
freshly squeezed juice	**jus peras**	[dʒʲus pəras]

beer	**bir**	[bir]
lager	**bir putih**	[bir putih]
bitter	**bir hitam**	[bir hitam]

tea	**teh**	[teh]
black tea	**teh hitam**	[teh hitam]
green tea	**teh hijau**	[teh hidʒʲau]

54. Vegetables

| vegetables | **sayuran** | [sajuran] |
| greens | **sayuran hijau** | [sajuran hidʒʲau] |

tomato	**tomat**	[tomat]
cucumber	**mentimun, ketimun**	[mentimun], [ketimun]
carrot	**wortel**	[wortel]
potato	**kentang**	[kentaŋ]
onion	**bawang**	[bawaŋ]
garlic	**bawang putih**	[bawaŋ putih]

| cabbage | **kol** | [kol] |
| cauliflower | **kembang kol** | [kembaŋ kol] |

| Brussels sprouts | **kol Brussels** | [kol brusels] |
| broccoli | **brokoli** | [brokoli] |

beetroot	**ubi bit merah**	[ubi bit merah]
aubergine	**terung, terong**	[teruŋ], [təroŋ]
courgette	**labu siam**	[labu siam]

| pumpkin | **labu** | [labu] |
| turnip | **turnip** | [turnip] |

parsley	**peterseli**	[peterseli]
dill	**adas sowa**	[adas sowa]
lettuce	**selada**	[selada]
celery	**seledri**	[seledri]

| asparagus | **asparagus** | [asparagus] |
| spinach | **bayam** | [bajam] |

| pea | **kacang polong** | [katʃaŋ poloŋ] |
| beans | **kacang-kacangan** | [katʃaŋ-katʃaŋan] |

| maize | **jagung** | [dʒʲaguŋ] |
| kidney bean | **kacang buncis** | [katʃaŋ buntʃis] |

sweet paper	**cabai**	[tʃabaj]
radish	**radis**	[radis]
artichoke	**artisyok**	[artiʃoʔ]

55. Fruits. Nuts

fruit	**buah**	[buah]
apple	**apel**	[apel]
pear	**pir**	[pir]
lemon	**jeruk sitrun**	[dʒˈeruʔ sitrun]
orange	**jeruk manis**	[dʒˈeruʔ manis]
strawberry (garden ~)	**stroberi**	[stroberi]
tangerine	**jeruk mandarin**	[dʒˈeruʔ mandarin]
plum	**plum**	[plum]
peach	**persik**	[persiʔ]
apricot	**aprikot**	[aprikot]
raspberry	**buah frambus**	[buah frambus]
pineapple	**nanas**	[nanas]
banana	**pisang**	[pisaŋ]
watermelon	**semangka**	[semaŋka]
grape	**buah anggur**	[buah aŋgur]
sour cherry	**buah ceri asam**	[buah tʃeri asam]
sweet cherry	**buah ceri manis**	[buah tʃeri manis]
melon	**melon**	[melon]
grapefruit	**jeruk Bali**	[dʒˈeruʔ bali]
avocado	**avokad**	[avokad]
papaya	**pepaya**	[pepaja]
mango	**mangga**	[maŋga]
pomegranate	**buah delima**	[buah delima]
redcurrant	**redcurrant**	[redkaren]
blackcurrant	**blackcurrant**	[bleʔkaren]
gooseberry	**buah arbei hijau**	[buah arbei hidʒˈau]
bilberry	**buah bilberi**	[buah bilberi]
blackberry	**beri hitam**	[beri hitam]
raisin	**kismis**	[kismis]
fig	**buah ara**	[buah ara]
date	**buah kurma**	[buah kurma]
peanut	**kacang tanah**	[katʃaŋ tanah]
almond	**badam**	[badam]
walnut	**buah walnut**	[buah walnut]
hazelnut	**kacang hazel**	[katʃaŋ hazel]
coconut	**buah kelapa**	[buah kelapa]
pistachios	**badam hijau**	[badam hidʒˈau]

56. Bread. Sweets

bakers' confectionery (pastry)	**kue-mue**	[kue-mue]
bread	**roti**	[roti]
biscuits	**biskuit**	[biskuit]
chocolate (n)	**cokelat**	[tʃokelat]
chocolate (as adj)	**cokelat**	[tʃokelat]

candy (wrapped)	**permen**	[pərmen]
cake (e.g. cupcake)	**kue**	[kue]
cake (e.g. birthday ~)	**kue tar**	[kue tar]

| pie (e.g. apple ~) | **pai** | [pai] |
| filling (for cake, pie) | **inti** | [inti] |

jam (whole fruit jam)	**selai buah utuh**	[selaj buah utuh]
marmalade	**marmelade**	[marmelade]
wafers	**wafel**	[wafel]
ice-cream	**es krim**	[es krim]
pudding (Christmas ~)	**puding**	[pudiŋ]

57. Spices

salt	**garam**	[garam]
salty (adj)	**asin**	[asin]
to salt (vt)	**menggarami**	[məŋgarami]

black pepper	**merica**	[meritʃa]
red pepper (milled ~)	**cabai merah**	[tʃabaj merah]
mustard	**mustar**	[mustar]
horseradish	**lobak pedas**	[loba' pedas]

condiment	**bumbu**	[bumbu]
spice	**rempah-rempah**	[rempah-rempah]
sauce	**saus**	[saus]
vinegar	**cuka**	[tʃuka]

anise	**adas manis**	[adas manis]
basil	**selasih**	[selasih]
cloves	**cengkih**	[tʃeŋkih]
ginger	**jahe**	[dʒʲahe]
coriander	**ketumbar**	[ketumbar]
cinnamon	**kayu manis**	[kaju manis]

sesame	**wijen**	[widʒʲen]
bay leaf	**daun salam**	[daun salam]
paprika	**cabai**	[tʃabaj]
caraway	**jintan**	[dʒintan]
saffron	**kuma-kuma**	[kuma-kuma]

PERSONAL INFORMATION. FAMILY

58. Personal information. Forms

name (first name)	nama, nama depan	[nama], [nama depan]
surname (last name)	nama keluarga	[nama keluarga]
date of birth	tanggal lahir	[taŋgal lahir]
place of birth	tempat lahir	[tempat lahir]
nationality	kebangsaan	[kebaŋsa'an]
place of residence	tempat tinggal	[tempat tiŋgal]
country	negara, negeri	[negara], [negeri]
profession (occupation)	profesi	[profesi]
gender, sex	jenis kelamin	[dʒenis kelamin]
height	tinggi badan	[tiŋgi badan]
weight	berat	[berat]

59. Family members. Relatives

mother	ibu	[ibu]
father	ayah	[ajah]
son	anak lelaki	[ana' lelaki]
daughter	anak perempuan	[ana' perempuan]
younger daughter	anak perempuan bungsu	[ana' perempuan buŋsu]
younger son	anak lelaki bungsu	[ana' lelaki buŋsu]
eldest daughter	anak perempuan sulung	[ana' perempuan suluŋ]
eldest son	anak lelaki sulung	[ana' lelaki suluŋ]
brother	saudara lelaki	[saudara lelaki]
elder brother	kakak lelaki	[kaka' lelaki]
younger brother	adik lelaki	[adi' lelaki]
sister	saudara perempuan	[saudara perempuan]
elder sister	kakak perempuan	[kaka' perempuan]
younger sister	adik perempuan	[adi' perempuan]
cousin (masc.)	sepupu lelaki	[sepupu lelaki]
cousin (fem.)	sepupu perempuan	[sepupu perempuan]
mummy	mama, ibu	[mama], [ibu]
dad, daddy	papa, ayah	[papa], [ajah]
parents	orang tua	[oraŋ tua]
child	anak	[ana']
children	anak-anak	[ana'-ana']
grandmother	nenek	[nene']
grandfather	kakek	[kake']

grandson	cucu laki-laki	[ʧuʧu laki-laki]
granddaughter	cucu perempuan	[ʧuʧu pərempuan]
grandchildren	cucu	[ʧuʧu]

uncle	paman	[paman]
aunt	bibi	[bibi]
nephew	keponakan laki-laki	[keponakan laki-laki]
niece	keponakan perempuan	[keponakan pərempuan]

mother-in-law (wife's mother)	ibu mertua	[ibu mertua]
father-in-law (husband's father)	ayah mertua	[ajah mertua]
son-in-law (daughter's husband)	menantu laki-laki	[mənantu laki-laki]
stepmother	ibu tiri	[ibu tiri]
stepfather	ayah tiri	[ajah tiri]

infant	bayi	[baji]
baby (infant)	bayi	[baji]
little boy, kid	bocah cilik	[boʧah ʧili']

wife	istri	[istri]
husband	suami	[suami]
spouse (husband)	suami	[suami]
spouse (wife)	istri	[istri]

married (masc.)	menikah, beristri	[mənikah], [bəristri]
married (fem.)	menikah, bersuami	[mənikah], [bərsuami]
single (unmarried)	bujang	[budʒˈaŋ]
bachelor	bujang	[budʒˈaŋ]
divorced (masc.)	bercerai	[bərʧeraj]
widow	janda	[dʒˈanda]
widower	duda	[duda]

relative	kerabat	[kerabat]
close relative	kerabat dekat	[kerabat dekat]
distant relative	kerabat jauh	[kerabat dʒˈauh]
relatives	kerabat, sanak saudara	[kerabat], [sana' saudara]

orphan (boy or girl)	yatim piatu	[yatim piatu]
guardian (of a minor)	wali	[wali]
to adopt (a boy)	mengadopsi	[məŋadopsi]
to adopt (a girl)	mengadopsi	[məŋadopsi]

60. Friends. Colleagues

friend (masc.)	sahabat	[sahabat]
friend (fem.)	sahabat	[sahabat]
friendship	persahabatan	[pərsahabatan]
to be friends	bersahabat	[bərsahabat]

| pal (masc.) | teman | [teman] |
| pal (fem.) | teman | [teman] |

partner	**mitra**	[mitra]
chief (boss)	**atasan**	[atasan]
superior (n)	**atasan**	[atasan]
owner, proprietor	**pemilik**	[pemiliˀ]
subordinate (n)	**bawahan**	[bawahan]
colleague	**kolega**	[kolega]

acquaintance (person)	**kenalan**	[kenalan]
fellow traveller	**rekan seperjalanan**	[rekan seperdʒalanan]
classmate	**teman sekelas**	[teman sekelas]

neighbour (masc.)	**tetangga**	[tetaŋga]
neighbour (fem.)	**tetangga**	[tetaŋga]
neighbours	**para tetangga**	[para tetaŋga]

HUMAN BODY. MEDICINE

61. Head

head	**kepala**	[kepala]
face	**wajah**	[waʤ'ah]
nose	**hidung**	[hiduŋ]
mouth	**mulut**	[mulut]
eye	**mata**	[mata]
eyes	**mata**	[mata]
pupil	**pupil, biji mata**	[pupil], [biʤi mata]
eyebrow	**alis**	[alis]
eyelash	**bulu mata**	[bulu mata]
eyelid	**kelopak mata**	[kelopaʔ mata]
tongue	**lidah**	[lidah]
tooth	**gigi**	[gigi]
lips	**bibir**	[bibir]
cheekbones	**tulang pipi**	[tulaŋ pipi]
gum	**gusi**	[gusi]
palate	**langit-langit mulut**	[laŋit-laŋit mulut]
nostrils	**lubang hidung**	[lubaŋ hiduŋ]
chin	**dagu**	[dagu]
jaw	**rahang**	[rahaŋ]
cheek	**pipi**	[pipi]
forehead	**dahi**	[dahi]
temple	**pelipis**	[pelipis]
ear	**telinga**	[teliŋa]
back of the head	**tengkuk**	[teŋkuʔ]
neck	**leher**	[leher]
throat	**tenggorok**	[teŋgoroʔ]
hair	**rambut**	[rambut]
hairstyle	**tatanan rambut**	[tatanan rambut]
haircut	**potongan rambut**	[potoŋan rambut]
wig	**wig, rambut palsu**	[wig], [rambut palsu]
moustache	**kumis**	[kumis]
beard	**janggut**	[ʤ'aŋgut]
to have (a beard, etc.)	**memelihara**	[memelihara]
plait	**kepang**	[kepaŋ]
sideboards	**brewok**	[brewoʔ]
red-haired (adj)	**merah pirang**	[merah piraŋ]
grey (hair)	**beruban**	[bəruban]
bald (adj)	**botak, plontos**	[botak], [plontos]
bald patch	**botak**	[botaʔ]

| ponytail | ekor kuda | [ekor kuda] |
| fringe | poni rambut | [poni rambut] |

62. Human body

| hand | tangan | [taŋan] |
| arm | lengan | [leŋan] |

finger	jari	[dʒˈari]
toe	jari	[dʒˈari]
thumb	jempol	[dʒˈempol]
little finger	jari kelingking	[dʒˈari keliŋkiŋ]
nail	kuku	[kuku]

fist	kepalan tangan	[kepalan taŋan]
palm	telapak	[telapaʔ]
wrist	pergelangan	[pərgelaŋan]
forearm	lengan bawah	[leŋan bawah]
elbow	siku	[siku]
shoulder	bahu	[bahu]

leg	kaki	[kaki]
foot	telapak kaki	[telapa' kaki]
knee	lutut	[lutut]
calf	betis	[betis]
hip	paha	[paha]
heel	tumit	[tumit]

body	tubuh	[tubuh]
stomach	perut	[perut]
chest	dada	[dada]
breast	payudara	[pajudara]
flank	rusuk	[rusuʔ]
back	punggung	[puŋguŋ]
lower back	pinggang bawah	[piŋgaŋ bawah]
waist	pinggang	[piŋgaŋ]

navel (belly button)	pusar	[pusar]
buttocks	pantat	[pantat]
bottom	pantat	[pantat]

beauty spot	tanda lahir	[tanda lahir]
birthmark (café au lait spot)	tanda lahir	[tanda lahir]
tattoo	tato	[tato]
scar	parut luka	[parut luka]

63. Diseases

illness	penyakit	[penjakit]
to be ill	sakit	[sakit]
health	kesehatan	[kesehatan]
runny nose (coryza)	hidung meler	[hiduŋ meler]

tonsillitis	radang tonsil	[radaŋ tonsil]
cold (illness)	pilek, selesma	[pilek], [selesma]
to catch a cold	masuk angin	[masu' aŋin]

bronchitis	bronkitis	[bronkitis]
pneumonia	radang paru-paru	[radaŋ paru-paru]
flu, influenza	flu	[flu]

shortsighted (adj)	rabun jauh	[rabun dʒ'auh]
longsighted (adj)	rabun dekat	[rabun dekat]
strabismus (crossed eyes)	mata juling	[mata dʒ'uliŋ]
squint-eyed (adj)	bermata juling	[bərmata dʒ'uliŋ]
cataract	katarak	[katara']
glaucoma	glaukoma	[glaukoma]

stroke	stroke	[stroke]
heart attack	infark	[infar']
myocardial infarction	serangan jantung	[seraŋan dʒ'antuŋ]
paralysis	kelumpuhan	[kelumpuhan]
to paralyse (vt)	melumpuhkan	[melumpuhkan]

allergy	alergi	[alergi]
asthma	asma	[asma]
diabetes	diabetes	[diabetes]

| toothache | sakit gigi | [sakit gigi] |
| caries | karies | [karies] |

diarrhoea	diare	[diarə]
constipation	konstipasi, sembelit	[konstipasi], [sembelit]
stomach upset	gangguan pencernaan	[gaŋuan pentʃarna'an]
food poisoning	keracunan makanan	[keratʃunan makanan]
to get food poisoning	keracunan makanan	[keratʃunan makanan]

arthritis	artritis	[artritis]
rickets	rakitis	[rakitis]
rheumatism	rematik	[remati']
atherosclerosis	aterosklerosis	[aterosklerosis]

gastritis	radang perut	[radaŋ pərut]
appendicitis	apendisitis	[apendisitis]
cholecystitis	radang pundi empedu	[radaŋ pundi empedu]
ulcer	tukak lambung	[tuka' lambuŋ]

measles	penyakit campak	[peɲakit tʃampa']
rubella (German measles)	penyakit campak Jerman	[peɲakit tʃampa' dʒ'erman]
jaundice	sakit kuning	[sakit kuniŋ]
hepatitis	hepatitis	[hepatitis]

schizophrenia	skizofrenia	[skizofrenia]
rabies (hydrophobia)	rabies	[rabies]
neurosis	neurosis	[neurosis]
concussion	gegar otak	[gegar ota']

| cancer | kanker | [kanker] |
| sclerosis | sklerosis | [sklerosis] |

multiple sclerosis	**sklerosis multipel**	[sklerosis multipel]
alcoholism	**alkoholisme**	[alkoholisme]
alcoholic (n)	**alkoholik**	[alkoholiʔ]
syphilis	**sifilis**	[sifilis]
AIDS	**AIDS**	[ajds]
tumour	**tumor**	[tumor]
malignant (adj)	**ganas**	[ganas]
benign (adj)	**jinak**	[dʒinaʔ]
fever	**demam**	[demam]
malaria	**malaria**	[malaria]
gangrene	**gangren**	[gaŋren]
seasickness	**mabuk laut**	[mabuʔ laut]
epilepsy	**epilepsi**	[epilepsi]
epidemic	**epidemi**	[epidemi]
typhus	**tifus**	[tifus]
tuberculosis	**tuberkulosis**	[tuberkulosis]
cholera	**kolera**	[kolera]
plague (bubonic ~)	**penyakit pes**	[penjakit pes]

64. Symptoms. Treatments. Part 1

symptom	**gejala**	[gedʒ'ala]
temperature	**temperatur, suhu**	[temperatur], [suhu]
high temperature (fever)	**temperatur tinggi**	[temperatur tiŋi]
pulse (heartbeat)	**denyut nadi**	[denyut nadi]
dizziness (vertigo)	**rasa pening**	[rasa peniŋ]
hot (adj)	**panas**	[panas]
shivering	**menggigil**	[meŋgigil]
pale (e.g. ~ face)	**pucat**	[putʃat]
cough	**batuk**	[batuʔ]
to cough (vi)	**batuk**	[batuʔ]
to sneeze (vi)	**bersin**	[bersin]
faint	**pingsan**	[piŋsan]
to faint (vi)	**jatuh pingsan**	[dʒ'atuh piŋsan]
bruise (hématome)	**luka memar**	[luka memar]
bump (lump)	**bengkak**	[beŋkaʔ]
to bang (bump)	**terantuk**	[terantuʔ]
contusion (bruise)	**luka memar**	[luka memar]
to get a bruise	**kena luka memar**	[kena luka memar]
to limp (vi)	**pincang**	[pintʃaŋ]
dislocation	**keseleo**	[keseleo]
to dislocate (vt)	**keseleo**	[keseleo]
fracture	**fraktura, patah tulang**	[fraktura], [patah tulaŋ]
to have a fracture	**patah tulang**	[patah tulaŋ]
cut (e.g. paper ~)	**teriris**	[teriris]
to cut oneself	**teriris**	[teriris]

bleeding	perdarahan	[pərdarahan]
burn (injury)	luka bakar	[luka bakar]
to get burned	menderita luka bakar	[mənderita luka bakar]

to prick (vt)	menusuk	[mənusuʔ]
to prick oneself	tertusuk	[tərtusuʔ]
to injure (vt)	melukai	[melukaj]
injury	cedera	[tʃedera]
wound	luka	[luka]
trauma	trauma	[trauma]

to be delirious	mengigau	[məŋigau]
to stutter (vi)	gagap	[gagap]
sunstroke	sengatan matahari	[seŋatan matahari]

65. Symptoms. Treatments. Part 2

| pain, ache | sakit | [sakit] |
| splinter (in foot, etc.) | selumbar | [selumbar] |

sweat (perspiration)	keringat	[keriŋat]
to sweat (perspire)	berkeringat	[bərkeriŋat]
vomiting	muntah	[muntah]
convulsions	kram	[kram]

pregnant (adj)	hamil	[hamil]
to be born	lahir	[lahir]
delivery, labour	persalinan	[pərsalinan]
to deliver (~ a baby)	melahirkan	[melahirkan]
abortion	aborsi	[aborsi]

breathing, respiration	pernapasan	[pərnapasan]
in-breath (inhalation)	tarikan napas	[tarikan napas]
out-breath (exhalation)	napas keluar	[napas keluar]
to exhale (breathe out)	mengembuskan napas	[məɲembuskan napas]
to inhale (vi)	menarik napas	[mənariʔ napas]

disabled person	penderita cacat	[penderita tʃatʃat]
cripple	penderita cacat	[penderita tʃatʃat]
drug addict	pecandu narkoba	[petʃandu narkoba]

deaf (adj)	tunarungu	[tunaruŋu]
mute (adj)	tunawicara	[tunawitʃara]
deaf mute (adj)	tunarungu-wicara	[tunaruŋu-witʃara]

mad, insane (adj)	gila	[gila]
madman	lelaki gila	[lelaki gila]
(demented person)		

| madwoman | perempuan gila | [perempuan gila] |
| to go insane | menggila | [məŋgila] |

gene	gen	[gen]
immunity	imunitas	[imunitas]
hereditary (adj)	turun-temurun	[turun-temurun]

congenital (adj)	**bawaan**	[bawa'an]
virus	**virus**	[virus]
microbe	**mikroba**	[mikroba]
bacterium	**bakteri**	[bakteri]
infection	**infeksi**	[infeksi]

66. Symptoms. Treatments. Part 3

hospital	**rumah sakit**	[rumah sakit]
patient	**pasien**	[pasien]
diagnosis	**diagnosis**	[diagnosis]
cure	**perawatan**	[pərawatan]
medical treatment	**pengobatan medis**	[peŋobatan medis]
to get treatment	**berobat**	[bərobat]
to treat (~ a patient)	**merawat**	[merawat]
to nurse (look after)	**merawat**	[merawat]
care (nursing ~)	**pengasuhan**	[peŋasuhan]
operation, surgery	**operasi, pembedahan**	[operasi], [pembedahan]
to bandage (head, limb)	**membalut**	[membalut]
bandaging	**pembalutan**	[pembalutan]
vaccination	**vaksinasi**	[vaksinasi]
to vaccinate (vt)	**memvaksinasi**	[memvaksinasi]
injection	**suntikan**	[suntikan]
to give an injection	**menyuntik**	[mənyunti']
attack	**serangan**	[seraŋan]
amputation	**amputasi**	[amputasi]
to amputate (vt)	**mengamputasi**	[məŋamputasi]
coma	**koma**	[koma]
to be in a coma	**dalam keadaan koma**	[dalam keada'an koma]
intensive care	**perawatan intensif**	[pərawatan intensif]
to recover (~ from flu)	**sembuh**	[sembuh]
condition (patient's ~)	**keadaan**	[keada'an]
consciousness	**kesadaran**	[kesadaran]
memory (faculty)	**memori, daya ingat**	[memori], [daja iŋat]
to pull out (tooth)	**mencabut**	[mentʃabut]
filling	**tambalan**	[tambalan]
to fill (a tooth)	**menambal**	[mənambal]
hypnosis	**hipnosis**	[hipnosis]
to hypnotize (vt)	**menghipnosis**	[məŋhipnosis]

67. Medicine. Drugs. Accessories

medicine, drug	**obat**	[obat]
remedy	**obat**	[obat]
to prescribe (vt)	**meresepkan**	[meresepkan]

prescription	**resep**	[resep]
tablet, pill	**pil, tablet**	[pil], [tablet]
ointment	**salep**	[salep]
ampoule	**ampul**	[ampul]
mixture, solution	**obat cair**	[obat tʃajr]
syrup	**sirop**	[sirop]
capsule	**pil**	[pil]
powder	**bubuk**	[bubuʔ]
gauze bandage	**perban**	[perban]
cotton wool	**kapas**	[kapas]
iodine	**iodium**	[iodium]
plaster	**plester obat**	[plester obat]
eyedropper	**tetes mata**	[tetes mata]
thermometer	**termometer**	[tərmometər]
syringe	**alat suntik**	[alat suntiʔ]
wheelchair	**kursi roda**	[kursi roda]
crutches	**kruk**	[kruʔ]
painkiller	**obat bius**	[obat bius]
laxative	**laksatif, obat pencuci perut**	[laksatif], [obat pentʃutʃi pərut]
spirits (ethanol)	**spiritus, alkohol**	[spiritus], [alkohol]
medicinal herbs	**tanaman obat**	[tanaman obat]
herbal (~ tea)	**herbal**	[herbal]

FLAT

68. Flat

flat	apartemen	[apartemen]
room	kamar	[kamar]
bedroom	kamar tidur	[kamar tidur]
dining room	ruang makan	[ruaŋ makan]
living room	ruang tamu	[ruaŋ tamu]
study (home office)	ruang kerja	[ruaŋ kerdʒʲa]
entry room	ruang depan	[ruaŋ depan]
bathroom	kamar mandi	[kamar mandi]
water closet	kamar kecil	[kamar ketʃil]
ceiling	plafon, langit-langit	[plafon], [laŋit-laŋit]
floor	lantai	[lantaj]
corner	sudut	[sudut]

69. Furniture. Interior

furniture	mebel	[mebel]
table	meja	[medʒʲa]
chair	kursi	[kursi]
bed	ranjang	[randʒʲaŋ]
sofa, settee	dipan	[dipan]
armchair	kursi malas	[kursi malas]
bookcase	lemari buku	[lemari buku]
shelf	rak	[raʔ]
wardrobe	lemari pakaian	[lemari pakajan]
coat rack (wall-mounted ~)	kapstok	[kapstoʔ]
coat stand	kapstok berdiri	[kapstoʔ bərdiri]
chest of drawers	lemari laci	[lemari latʃi]
coffee table	meja kopi	[medʒʲa kopi]
mirror	cermin	[tʃermin]
carpet	permadani	[pərmadani]
small carpet	karpet kecil	[karpet ketʃil]
fireplace	perapian	[pərapian]
candle	lilin	[lilin]
candlestick	kaki lilin	[kaki lilin]
drapes	gorden	[gorden]
wallpaper	kertas dinding	[kertas dindiŋ]

blinds (jalousie)	**kerai**	[keraj]
table lamp	**lampu meja**	[lampu medʒia]
wall lamp (sconce)	**lampu dinding**	[lampu dindiŋ]
standard lamp	**lampu lantai**	[lampu lantaj]
chandelier	**lampu bercabang**	[lampu bərtʃabaŋ]
leg (of a chair, table)	**kaki**	[kaki]
armrest	**lengan**	[leŋan]
back (backrest)	**sandaran**	[sandaran]
drawer	**laci**	[latʃi]

70. Bedding

bedclothes	**kain kasur**	[kain kasur]
pillow	**bantal**	[bantal]
pillowslip	**sarung bantal**	[saruŋ bantal]
duvet	**selimut**	[selimut]
sheet	**seprai**	[sepraj]
bedspread	**selubung kasur**	[selubuŋ kasur]

71. Kitchen

kitchen	**dapur**	[dapur]
gas	**gas**	[gas]
gas cooker	**kompor gas**	[kompor gas]
electric cooker	**kompor listrik**	[kompor listriʔ]
oven	**oven**	[oven]
microwave oven	**microwave**	[majkrowav]
refrigerator	**lemari es, kulkas**	[lemari es], [kulkas]
freezer	**lemari pembeku**	[lemari pembeku]
dishwasher	**mesin pencuci piring**	[mesin pentʃutʃi piriŋ]
mincer	**alat pelumat daging**	[alat pelumat dagiŋ]
juicer	**mesin sari buah**	[mesin sari buah]
toaster	**alat pemanggang roti**	[alat pemaŋgaŋ roti]
mixer	**pencampur**	[pentʃampur]
coffee machine	**mesin pembuat kopi**	[mesin pembuat kopi]
coffee pot	**teko kopi**	[teko kopi]
coffee grinder	**mesin penggiling kopi**	[mesin peŋgiliŋ kopi]
kettle	**cerek**	[tʃereʔ]
teapot	**teko**	[teko]
lid	**tutup**	[tutup]
tea strainer	**saringan teh**	[sariŋan teh]
spoon	**sendok**	[sendoʔ]
teaspoon	**sendok teh**	[sendoʔ teh]
soup spoon	**sendok makan**	[sendoʔ makan]
fork	**garpu**	[garpu]
knife	**pisau**	[pisau]

tableware (dishes)	**piring mangkuk**	[piriŋ maŋkuʔ]
plate (dinner ~)	**piring**	[piriŋ]
saucer	**alas cangkir**	[alas ʧaŋkir]

shot glass	**seloki**	[seloki]
glass (tumbler)	**gelas**	[gelas]
cup	**cangkir**	[ʧaŋkir]

sugar bowl	**wadah gula**	[wadah gula]
salt cellar	**wadah garam**	[wadah garam]
pepper pot	**wadah merica**	[wadah meriʧa]
butter dish	**wadah mentega**	[wadah mentega]

stock pot (soup pot)	**panci**	[panʧi]
frying pan (skillet)	**kuali**	[kuali]
ladle	**sudu**	[sudu]
colander	**saringan**	[sariŋan]
tray (serving ~)	**talam**	[talam]

bottle	**botol**	[botol]
jar (glass)	**gelas**	[gelas]
tin (can)	**kaleng**	[kaleŋ]

bottle opener	**pembuka botol**	[pembuka botol]
tin opener	**pembuka kaleng**	[pembuka kaleŋ]
corkscrew	**kotrek**	[kotreʔ]
filter	**saringan**	[sariŋan]
to filter (vt)	**saringan**	[sariŋan]

| waste (food ~, etc.) | **sampah** | [sampah] |
| waste bin (kitchen ~) | **tong sampah** | [toŋ sampah] |

72. Bathroom

bathroom	**kamar mandi**	[kamar mandi]
water	**air**	[air]
tap	**keran**	[keran]
hot water	**air panas**	[air panas]
cold water	**air dingin**	[air diŋin]

toothpaste	**pasta gigi**	[pasta gigi]
to clean one's teeth	**menggosok gigi**	[məŋgosoʔ gigi]
toothbrush	**sikat gigi**	[sikat gigi]

to shave (vi)	**bercukur**	[berʧukur]
shaving foam	**busa cukur**	[busa ʧukur]
razor	**pisau cukur**	[pisau ʧukur]

to wash (one's hands, etc.)	**mencuci**	[mənʧuʧi]
to have a bath	**mandi**	[mandi]
shower	**pancuran**	[panʧuran]
to have a shower	**mandi pancuran**	[mandi panʧuran]
bath	**bak mandi**	[baʔ mandi]
toilet (toilet bowl)	**kloset**	[kloset]

sink (washbasin)	wastafel	[wastafel]
soap	sabun	[sabun]
soap dish	wadah sabun	[wadah sabun]

sponge	spons	[spons]
shampoo	sampo	[sampo]
towel	handuk	[handuʔ]
bathrobe	jubah mandi	[dʒᵘubah mandi]

laundry (laundering)	pencucian	[pentʃutʃian]
washing machine	mesin cuci	[mesin tʃutʃi]
to do the laundry	mencuci	[məntʃutʃi]
washing powder	deterjen cuci	[deterdʒᵉen tʃutʃi]

73. Household appliances

TV, telly	pesawat TV	[pesawat ti-vi]
tape recorder	alat perekam	[alat pərekam]
video	video, VCR	[vidio], [vi-si-er]
radio	radio	[radio]
player (CD, MP3, etc.)	pemutar	[pemutar]

video projector	proyektor video	[proektor video]
home cinema	bioskop rumah	[bioskop rumah]
DVD player	pemutar DVD	[pemutar di-vi-di]
amplifier	penguat	[pəŋuat]
video game console	konsol permainan video	[konsol pərmajnan video]

video camera	kamera video	[kamera video]
camera (photo)	kamera	[kamera]
digital camera	kamera digital	[kamera digital]

vacuum cleaner	pengisap debu	[pəŋisap debu]
iron (e.g. steam ~)	setrika	[setrika]
ironing board	papan setrika	[papan setrika]

telephone	telepon	[telepon]
mobile phone	ponsel	[ponsel]
typewriter	mesin ketik	[mesin ketiʔ]
sewing machine	mesin jahit	[mesin dʒᵘahit]

microphone	mikrofon	[mikrofon]
headphones	headphone, fonkepala	[headphone], [fonkepala]
remote control (TV)	panel kendali	[panel kendali]

CD, compact disc	cakram kompak	[tʃakram kompaʔ]
cassette, tape	kaset	[kaset]
vinyl record	piringan hitam	[piriŋan hitam]

THE EARTH. WEATHER

74. Outer space

space	angkasa	[aŋkasa]
space (as adj)	angkasa	[aŋkasa]
outer space	ruang angkasa	[ruaŋ aŋkasa]
world	dunia	[dunia]
universe	jagat raya	[dʒjagat raja]
galaxy	galaksi	[galaksi]
star	bintang	[bintaŋ]
constellation	gugusan bintang	[gugusan bintaŋ]
planet	planet	[planet]
satellite	satelit	[satelit]
meteorite	meteorit	[meteorit]
comet	komet	[komet]
asteroid	asteroid	[asteroid]
orbit	orbit	[orbit]
to revolve	berputar	[berputar]
(~ around the Earth)		
atmosphere	atmosfer	[atmosfer]
the Sun	matahari	[matahari]
solar system	tata surya	[tata surja]
solar eclipse	gerhana matahari	[gerhana matahari]
the Earth	Bumi	[bumi]
the Moon	Bulan	[bulan]
Mars	Mars	[mars]
Venus	Venus	[venus]
Jupiter	Yupiter	[yupiter]
Saturn	Saturnus	[saturnus]
Mercury	Merkurius	[merkurius]
Uranus	Uranus	[uranus]
Neptune	Neptunus	[neptunus]
Pluto	Pluto	[pluto]
Milky Way	Bimasakti	[bimasakti]
Great Bear (Ursa Major)	Ursa Major	[ursa madʒor]
North Star	Bintang Utara	[bintaŋ utara]
Martian	makhluk Mars	[mahluʾ mars]
extraterrestrial (n)	makhluk ruang angkasa	[mahluʾ ruaŋ aŋkasa]
alien	alien, makhluk asing	[alien], [mahluʾ asiŋ]

flying saucer	piring terbang	[piriŋ tərban]
spaceship	kapal antariksa	[kapal antariksa]
space station	stasiun antariksa	[stasiun antariksa]
blast-off	peluncuran	[peluntʃuran]
engine	mesin	[mesin]
nozzle	nosel	[nosel]
fuel	bahan bakar	[bahan bakar]
cockpit, flight deck	kokpit	[kokpit]
aerial	antena	[antena]
porthole	jendela	[dʒʲendela]
solar panel	sel surya	[sel surja]
spacesuit	pakaian antariksa	[pakajan antariksa]
weightlessness	keadaan tanpa bobot	[keada'an tanpa bobot]
oxygen	oksigen	[oksigen]
docking (in space)	penggabungan	[peŋgabuŋan]
to dock (vi, vt)	bergabung	[bərgabuŋ]
observatory	observatorium	[observatorium]
telescope	teleskop	[teleskop]
to observe (vt)	mengamati	[məŋamati]
to explore (vt)	mengeksplorasi	[məŋeksplorasi]

75. The Earth

the Earth	Bumi	[bumi]
the globe (the Earth)	bola Bumi	[bola bumi]
planet	planet	[planet]
atmosphere	atmosfer	[atmosfer]
geography	geografi	[geografi]
nature	alam	[alam]
globe (table ~)	globe	[globe]
map	peta	[peta]
atlas	atlas	[atlas]
Europe	Eropa	[eropa]
Asia	Asia	[asia]
Africa	Afrika	[afrika]
Australia	Australia	[australia]
America	Amerika	[amerika]
North America	Amerika Utara	[amerika utara]
South America	Amerika Selatan	[amerika selatan]
Antarctica	Antartika	[antartika]
the Arctic	Arktika	[arktika]

76. Cardinal directions

north	**utara**	[utara]
to the north	**ke utara**	[ke utara]
in the north	**di utara**	[di utara]
northern (adj)	**utara**	[utara]
south	**selatan**	[selatan]
to the south	**ke selatan**	[ke selatan]
in the south	**di selatan**	[di selatan]
southern (adj)	**selatan**	[selatan]
west	**barat**	[barat]
to the west	**ke barat**	[ke barat]
in the west	**di barat**	[di barat]
western (adj)	**barat**	[barat]
east	**timur**	[timur]
to the east	**ke timur**	[ke timur]
in the east	**di timur**	[di timur]
eastern (adj)	**timur**	[timur]

77. Sea. Ocean

sea	**laut**	[laut]
ocean	**samudra**	[samudra]
gulf (bay)	**teluk**	[teluʔ]
straits	**selat**	[selat]
land (solid ground)	**daratan**	[daratan]
continent (mainland)	**benua**	[benua]
island	**pulau**	[pulau]
peninsula	**semenanjung, jazirah**	[semenandʒʲuŋ], [dʒʲazirah]
archipelago	**kepulauan**	[kepulauan]
bay, cove	**teluk**	[teluʔ]
harbour	**pelabuhan**	[pelabuhan]
lagoon	**laguna**	[laguna]
cape	**tanjung**	[tandʒʲuŋ]
atoll	**pulau karang**	[pulau karaŋ]
reef	**terumbu**	[terumbu]
coral	**karang**	[karaŋ]
coral reef	**terumbu karang**	[terumbu karaŋ]
deep (adj)	**dalam**	[dalam]
depth (deep water)	**kedalaman**	[kedalaman]
abyss	**jurang**	[dʒʲuraŋ]
trench (e.g. Mariana ~)	**palung**	[paluŋ]
current (Ocean ~)	**arus**	[arus]
to surround (bathe)	**berbatasan dengan**	[berbatasan deŋan]

shore	**pantai**	[pantaj]
coast	**pantai**	[pantaj]
flow (flood tide)	**air pasang**	[air pasaŋ]
ebb (ebb tide)	**air surut**	[air surut]
shoal	**beting**	[betiŋ]
bottom (~ of the sea)	**dasar**	[dasar]
wave	**gelombang**	[gelombaŋ]
crest (~ of a wave)	**puncak gelombang**	[puntʃa' gelombaŋ]
spume (sea foam)	**busa, buih**	[busa], [buih]
storm (sea storm)	**badai**	[badaj]
hurricane	**topan**	[topan]
tsunami	**tsunami**	[tsunami]
calm (dead ~)	**angin tenang**	[aŋin tenaŋ]
quiet, calm (adj)	**tenang**	[tenaŋ]
pole	**kutub**	[kutub]
polar (adj)	**kutub**	[kutub]
latitude	**lintang**	[lintaŋ]
longitude	**garis bujur**	[garis budʒʲur]
parallel	**sejajar**	[sedʒʲadʒʲar]
equator	**khatulistiwa**	[hatulistiwa]
sky	**langit**	[laŋit]
horizon	**horizon**	[horizon]
air	**udara**	[udara]
lighthouse	**mercusuar**	[mertʃusuar]
to dive (vi)	**menyelam**	[mənjelam]
to sink (ab. boat)	**karam**	[karam]
treasure	**harta karun**	[harta karun]

78. Seas & Oceans names

Atlantic Ocean	**Samudra Atlantik**	[samudra atlanti']
Indian Ocean	**Samudra Hindia**	[samudra hindia]
Pacific Ocean	**Samudra Pasifik**	[samudra pasifi']
Arctic Ocean	**Samudra Arktik**	[samudra arkti']
Black Sea	**Laut Hitam**	[laut hitam]
Red Sea	**Laut Merah**	[laut merah]
Yellow Sea	**Laut Kuning**	[laut kuniŋ]
White Sea	**Laut Putih**	[laut putih]
Caspian Sea	**Laut Kaspia**	[laut kaspia]
Dead Sea	**Laut Mati**	[laut mati]
Mediterranean Sea	**Laut Tengah**	[laut teŋah]
Aegean Sea	**Laut Aegean**	[laut aegean]
Adriatic Sea	**Laut Adriatik**	[laut adriati']
Arabian Sea	**Laut Arab**	[laut arab]

Sea of Japan	**Laut Jepang**	[laut dʒ'epaŋ]
Bering Sea	**Laut Bering**	[laut beriŋ]
South China Sea	**Laut Cina Selatan**	[laut tʃina selatan]
Coral Sea	**Laut Karang**	[laut karaŋ]
Tasman Sea	**Laut Tasmania**	[laut tasmania]
Caribbean Sea	**Laut Karibia**	[laut karibia]
Barents Sea	**Laut Barents**	[laut barents]
Kara Sea	**Laut Kara**	[laut kara]
North Sea	**Laut Utara**	[laut utara]
Baltic Sea	**Laut Baltik**	[laut balti']
Norwegian Sea	**Laut Norwegia**	[laut norwegia]

79. Mountains

mountain	**gunung**	[gunuŋ]
mountain range	**jajaran gunung**	[dʒ'adʒ'aran gunuŋ]
mountain ridge	**sisir gunung**	[sisir gunuŋ]
summit, top	**puncak**	[puntʃa']
peak	**puncak**	[puntʃa']
foot (~ of the mountain)	**kaki**	[kaki]
slope (mountainside)	**lereng**	[lereŋ]
volcano	**gunung api**	[gunuŋ api]
active volcano	**gunung api yang aktif**	[gunuŋ api yaŋ aktif]
dormant volcano	**gunung api yang tidak aktif**	[gunuŋ api yaŋ tida' aktif]
eruption	**erupsi, letusan**	[erupsi], [letusan]
crater	**kawah**	[kawah]
magma	**magma**	[magma]
lava	**lava, lahar**	[lava], [lahar]
molten (~ lava)	**pijar**	[pidʒ'ar]
canyon	**kanyon**	[kanjon]
gorge	**jurang**	[dʒ'uraŋ]
crevice	**celah**	[tʃelah]
abyss (chasm)	**jurang**	[dʒ'uraŋ]
pass, col	**pass, celah**	[pass], [tʃelah]
plateau	**plato, dataran tinggi**	[plato], [dataran tiŋgi]
cliff	**tebing**	[tebiŋ]
hill	**bukit**	[bukit]
glacier	**gletser**	[gletser]
waterfall	**air terjun**	[air terdʒ'un]
geyser	**geiser**	[geyser]
lake	**danau**	[danau]
plain	**dataran**	[dataran]
landscape	**landskap**	[landskap]
echo	**gema**	[gema]

alpinist	**pendaki gunung**	[pendaki gunuŋ]
rock climber	**pemanjat tebing**	[pemandʒat tebiŋ]
to conquer (in climbing)	**menaklukkan**	[mənakluʔkan]
climb (an easy ~)	**pendakian**	[pendakian]

80. Mountains names

The Alps	**Alpen**	[alpen]
Mont Blanc	**Mont Blanc**	[mon blan]
The Pyrenees	**Pirenia**	[pirenia]
The Carpathians	**Pegunungan Karpatia**	[pegununaŋ karpatia]
The Ural Mountains	**Pegunungan Ural**	[pegununaŋ ural]
The Caucasus Mountains	**Kaukasus**	[kaukasus]
Mount Elbrus	**Elbrus**	[elbrus]
The Altai Mountains	**Altai**	[altaj]
The Tian Shan	**Tien Shan**	[tjen ʃan]
The Pamirs	**Pegunungan Pamir**	[pegununaŋ pamir]
The Himalayas	**Himalaya**	[himalaja]
Mount Everest	**Everest**	[everest]
The Andes	**Andes**	[andes]
Mount Kilimanjaro	**Kilimanjaro**	[kilimandʒaro]

81. Rivers

river	**sungai**	[suŋaj]
spring (natural source)	**mata air**	[mata air]
riverbed (river channel)	**badan sungai**	[badan suŋaj]
basin (river valley)	**basin**	[basin]
to flow into ...	**mengalir ke ...**	[məŋalir ke ...]
tributary	**anak sungai**	[anaʔ suŋaj]
bank (river ~)	**tebing sungai**	[tebiŋ suŋaj]
current (stream)	**arus**	[arus]
downstream (adv)	**ke hilir**	[ke hilir]
upstream (adv)	**ke hulu**	[ke hulu]
inundation	**banjir**	[bandʒir]
flooding	**banjir**	[bandʒir]
to overflow (vi)	**membanjiri**	[membandʒiri]
to flood (vt)	**membanjiri**	[membandʒiri]
shallow (shoal)	**beting**	[betiŋ]
rapids	**jeram**	[dʒeram]
dam	**dam, bendungan**	[dam], [bendunaŋ]
canal	**kanal, terusan**	[kanal], [tərusan]
reservoir (artificial lake)	**waduk**	[waduʔ]
sluice, lock	**pintu air**	[pintu air]

water body (pond, etc.)	**kolam**	[kolam]
swamp (marshland)	**rawa**	[rawa]
bog, marsh	**bencah, paya**	[bentʃah], [paja]
whirlpool	**pusaran air**	[pusaran air]
stream (brook)	**selokan**	[selokan]
drinking (ab. water)	**minum**	[minum]
fresh (~ water)	**tawar**	[tawar]
ice	**es**	[es]
to freeze over (ab. river, etc.)	**membeku**	[membeku]

82. Rivers names

Seine	**Seine**	[seine]
Loire	**Loire**	[loire]
Thames	**Thames**	[tems]
Rhine	**Rein**	[reyn]
Danube	**Donau**	[donau]
Volga	**Volga**	[volga]
Don	**Don**	[don]
Lena	**Lena**	[lena]
Yellow River	**Suang Kuning**	[suaŋ kuniŋ]
Yangtze	**Yangtze**	[yaŋtze]
Mekong	**Mekong**	[mekoŋ]
Ganges	**Gangga**	[gaŋga]
Nile River	**Sungai Nil**	[suŋaj nil]
Congo River	**Kongo**	[koŋo]
Okavango River	**Okavango**	[okavaŋo]
Zambezi River	**Zambezi**	[zambezi]
Limpopo River	**Limpopo**	[limpopo]
Mississippi River	**Mississippi**	[misisipi]

83. Forest

forest, wood	**hutan**	[hutan]
forest (as adj)	**hutan**	[hutan]
thick forest	**hutan lebat**	[hutan lebat]
grove	**hutan kecil**	[hutan ketʃil]
forest clearing	**pembukaan hutan**	[pembuka'an hutan]
thicket	**semak belukar**	[sema' belukar]
scrubland	**belukar**	[belukar]
footpath (troddenpath)	**jalan setapak**	[dʒ'alan setapa']
gully	**parit**	[parit]
tree	**pohon**	[pohon]

leaf	**daun**	[daun]
leaves (foliage)	**daun-daunan**	[daun-daunan]
fall of leaves	**daun berguguran**	[daun bərguguran]
to fall (ab. leaves)	**luruh**	[luruh]
top (of the tree)	**puncak**	[puntʃaʔ]
branch	**cabang**	[tʃabaŋ]
bough	**dahan**	[dahan]
bud (on shrub, tree)	**tunas**	[tunas]
needle (of the pine tree)	**daun jarum**	[daun dʒ¡arum]
fir cone	**buah pinus**	[buah pinus]
tree hollow	**lubang pohon**	[lubaŋ pohon]
nest	**sarang**	[saraŋ]
burrow (animal hole)	**lubang**	[lubaŋ]
trunk	**batang**	[bataŋ]
root	**akar**	[akar]
bark	**kulit**	[kulit]
moss	**lumut**	[lumut]
to uproot (remove trees or tree stumps)	**mencabut**	[məntʃabut]
to chop down	**menebang**	[mənebaŋ]
to deforest (vt)	**deforestasi, penggundulan hutan**	[deforestasi, pəŋgundulan hutan]
tree stump	**tunggul**	[tuŋgul]
campfire	**api unggun**	[api uŋgun]
forest fire	**kebakaran hutan**	[kebakaran hutan]
to extinguish (vt)	**memadamkan**	[memadamkan]
forest ranger	**penjaga hutan**	[pendʒ¡aga hutan]
protection	**perlindungan**	[pərlinduŋan]
to protect (~ nature)	**melindungi**	[melinduŋi]
poacher	**pemburu ilegal**	[pemburu ilegal]
steel trap	**perangkap**	[pəraŋkap]
to gather, to pick (vt)	**memetik**	[memetiʔ]
to lose one's way	**tersesat**	[tərsesat]

84. Natural resources

natural resources	**sumber daya alam**	[sumber daja alam]
minerals	**bahan tambang**	[bahan tambaŋ]
deposits	**endapan**	[endapan]
field (e.g. oilfield)	**ladang**	[ladaŋ]
to mine (extract)	**menambang**	[mənambaŋ]
mining (extraction)	**pertambangan**	[pərtambaŋan]
ore	**bijih**	[bidʒih]
mine (e.g. for coal)	**tambang**	[tambaŋ]
shaft (mine ~)	**sumur tambang**	[sumur tambaŋ]

miner	penambang	[penambaŋ]
gas (natural ~)	gas	[gas]
gas pipeline	pipa saluran gas	[pipa saluran gas]

oil (petroleum)	petroleum, minyak	[petroleum], [minjaʔ]
oil pipeline	pipa saluran minyak	[pipa saluran minjaʔ]
oil well	sumur minyak	[sumur minjaʔ]
derrick (tower)	menara bor minyak	[mənara bor minjaʔ]
tanker	kapal tangki	[kapal taŋki]

sand	pasir	[pasir]
limestone	batu kapur	[batu kapur]
gravel	kerikil	[kerikil]
peat	gambut	[gambut]
clay	tanah liat	[tanah liat]
coal	arang	[araŋ]

iron (ore)	besi	[besi]
gold	emas	[emas]
silver	perak	[peraʔ]
nickel	nikel	[nikel]
copper	tembaga	[tembaga]

zinc	seng	[seŋ]
manganese	mangan	[maŋan]
mercury	air raksa	[air raksa]
lead	timbal	[timbal]

mineral	mineral	[mineral]
crystal	kristal, hablur	[kristal], [hablur]
marble	marmer	[marmer]
uranium	uranium	[uranium]

85. Weather

weather	cuaca	[ʧuaʧa]
weather forecast	prakiraan cuaca	[prakiraʔan ʧuaʧa]
temperature	temperatur, suhu	[temperatur], [suhu]
thermometer	termometer	[tərmometər]
barometer	barometer	[barometer]

| humid (adj) | lembap | [lembap] |
| humidity | kelembapan | [kelembapan] |

heat (extreme ~)	panas, gerah	[panas], [gerah]
hot (torrid)	panas terik	[panas teriʔ]
it's hot	panas	[panas]

| it's warm | hangat | [haŋat] |
| warm (moderately hot) | hangat | [haŋat] |

it's cold	dingin	[diŋin]
cold (adj)	dingin	[diŋin]
sun	matahari	[matahari]

to shine (vi)	bersinar	[bersinar]
sunny (day)	cerah	[tʃerah]
to come up (vi)	terbit	[terbit]
to set (vi)	terbenam	[terbenam]

cloud	awan	[awan]
cloudy (adj)	berawan	[berawan]
rain cloud	awan mendung	[awan menduŋ]
somber (gloomy)	mendung	[menduŋ]

rain	hujan	[hudʒ'an]
it's raining	hujan turun	[hudʒ'an turun]
rainy (~ day, weather)	hujan	[hudʒ'an]
to drizzle (vi)	gerimis	[gerimis]

pouring rain	hujan lebat	[hudʒ'an lebat]
downpour	hujan lebat	[hudʒ'an lebat]
heavy (e.g. ~ rain)	lebat	[lebat]
puddle	kubangan	[kubaŋan]
to get wet (in rain)	kehujanan	[kehudʒ'anan]

fog (mist)	kabut	[kabut]
foggy	berkabut	[berkabut]
snow	salju	[sald'ʒu]
it's snowing	turun salju	[turun sald'ʒu]

86. Severe weather. Natural disasters

thunderstorm	hujan badai	[hudʒ'an badaj]
lightning (~ strike)	kilat	[kilat]
to flash (vi)	berkilau	[berkilau]

thunder	petir	[petir]
to thunder (vi)	bergemuruh	[bergemuruh]
it's thundering	bergemuruh	[bergemuruh]

hail	hujan es	[hudʒ'an es]
it's hailing	hujan es	[hudʒ'an es]

to flood (vt)	membanjiri	[membandʒiri]
flood, inundation	banjir	[bandʒir]

earthquake	gempa bumi	[gempa bumi]
tremor, shoke	gempa	[gempa]
epicentre	episentrum	[episentrum]

eruption	erupsi, letusan	[erupsi], [letusan]
lava	lava, lahar	[lava], [lahar]

twister	puting beliung	[putiŋ beliuŋ]
tornado	tornado	[tornado]
typhoon	topan	[topan]
hurricane	topan	[topan]
storm	badai	[badaj]

tsunami	**tsunami**	[tsunami]
cyclone	**siklon**	[siklon]
bad weather	**cuaca buruk**	[ʧuaʧa buruʔ]
fire (accident)	**kebakaran**	[kebakaran]
disaster	**bencana**	[benʧana]
meteorite	**meteorit**	[meteorit]
avalanche	**longsor**	[loŋsor]
snowslide	**salju longsor**	[saldʒʲu loŋsor]
blizzard	**badai salju**	[badaj saldʒʲu]
snowstorm	**badai salju**	[badaj saldʒʲu]

FAUNA

87. Mammals. Predators

predator	**predator, pemangsa**	[predator], [pemaŋsa]
tiger	**harimau**	[harimau]
lion	**singa**	[siŋa]
wolf	**serigala**	[serigala]
fox	**rubah**	[rubah]
jaguar	**jaguar**	[dʒiaguar]
leopard	**leopard, macan tutul**	[leopard], [matʃan tutul]
cheetah	**cheetah**	[tʃeetah]
black panther	**harimau kumbang**	[harimau kumbaŋ]
puma	**singa gunung**	[siŋa gunuŋ]
snow leopard	**harimau bintang salju**	[harimau bintaŋ saldʒiu]
lynx	**lynx**	[links]
coyote	**koyote**	[koyot]
jackal	**jakal**	[dʒiakal]
hyena	**hiena**	[hiena]

88. Wild animals

animal	**binatang**	[binataŋ]
beast (animal)	**binatang buas**	[binataŋ buas]
squirrel	**bajing**	[badʒiŋ]
hedgehog	**landak susu**	[landa' susu]
hare	**terwelu**	[terwelu]
rabbit	**kelinci**	[kelintʃi]
badger	**luak**	[lua']
raccoon	**rakun**	[rakun]
hamster	**hamster**	[hamster]
marmot	**marmut**	[marmut]
mole	**tikus mondok**	[tikus mondo']
mouse	**tikus**	[tikus]
rat	**tikus besar**	[tikus besar]
bat	**kelelawar**	[kelelawar]
ermine	**ermin**	[ermin]
sable	**sabel**	[sabel]
marten	**marten**	[marten]
weasel	**musang**	[musaŋ]
mink	**cerpelai**	[tʃerpelai]

beaver	beaver	[beaver]
otter	berang-berang	[bəraŋ-bəraŋ]
horse	kuda	[kuda]
moose	rusa besar	[rusa besar]
deer	rusa	[rusa]
camel	unta	[unta]
bison	bison	[bison]
wisent	aurochs	[oroks]
buffalo	kerbau	[kerbau]
zebra	kuda belang	[kuda belaŋ]
antelope	antelop	[antelop]
roe deer	kijang	[kidʒʲaŋ]
fallow deer	rusa	[rusa]
chamois	chamois	[ʃemva]
wild boar	babi hutan jantan	[babi hutan dʒʲantan]
whale	ikan paus	[ikan paus]
seal	anjing laut	[andʒiŋ laut]
walrus	walrus	[walrus]
fur seal	anjing laut berbulu	[andʒiŋ laut berbulu]
dolphin	lumba-lumba	[lumba-lumba]
bear	beruang	[bəruaŋ]
polar bear	beruang kutub	[bəruaŋ kutub]
panda	panda	[panda]
monkey	monyet	[monjet]
chimpanzee	simpanse	[simpanse]
orangutan	orang utan	[oraŋ utan]
gorilla	gorila	[gorila]
macaque	kera	[kera]
gibbon	siamang, ungka	[siamaŋ], [uŋka]
elephant	gajah	[gadʒʲah]
rhinoceros	badak	[badaʔ]
giraffe	jerapah	[dʒʲerapah]
hippopotamus	kuda nil	[kuda nil]
kangaroo	kanguru	[kaŋuru]
koala (bear)	koala	[koala]
mongoose	garangan	[garaŋan]
chinchilla	chinchilla	[ʧinʧilla]
skunk	sigung	[siguŋ]
porcupine	landak	[landaʔ]

89. Domestic animals

cat	kucing betina	[kuʧiŋ betina]
tomcat	kucing jantan	[kuʧiŋ dʒʲantan]
dog	anjing	[andʒiŋ]

horse	kuda	[kuda]
stallion (male horse)	kuda jantan	[kuda dʒʲantan]
mare	kuda betina	[kuda betina]

cow	sapi	[sapi]
bull	sapi jantan	[sapi dʒʲantan]
ox	lembu jantan	[lembu dʒʲantan]

sheep (ewe)	domba	[domba]
ram	domba jantan	[domba dʒʲantan]
goat	kambing betina	[kambiŋ betina]
billy goat, he-goat	kambing jantan	[kambiŋ dʒʲantan]

| donkey | keledai | [keledaj] |
| mule | bagal | [bagal] |

pig	babi	[babi]
piglet	anak babi	[anaʔ babi]
rabbit	kelinci	[kelintʃi]

| hen (chicken) | ayam betina | [ajam betina] |
| cock | ayam jago | [ajam dʒʲago] |

duck	bebek	[bebeʔ]
drake	bebek jantan	[bebeʔ dʒʲantan]
goose	angsa	[aŋsa]

| tom turkey, gobbler | kalkun jantan | [kalkun dʒʲantan] |
| turkey (hen) | kalkun betina | [kalkun betina] |

domestic animals	binatang piaraan	[binataŋ piaraʔan]
tame (e.g. ~ hamster)	jinak	[dʒinaʔ]
to tame (vt)	menjinakkan	[məndʒinaʔkan]
to breed (vt)	membiakkan	[membiaʔkan]

farm	peternakan	[peternakan]
poultry	unggas	[uŋgas]
cattle	ternak	[ternaʔ]
herd (cattle)	kawanan	[kawanan]

stable	kandang kuda	[kandaŋ kuda]
pigsty	kandang babi	[kandaŋ babi]
cowshed	kandang sapi	[kandaŋ sapi]
rabbit hutch	sangkar kelinci	[saŋkar kelintʃi]
hen house	kandang ayam	[kandaŋ ajam]

90. Birds

bird	burung	[buruŋ]
pigeon	burung dara	[buruŋ dara]
sparrow	burung gereja	[buruŋ geredʒʲa]
tit (great tit)	burung tit	[buruŋ tit]
magpie	burung murai	[buruŋ muraj]
raven	burung raven	[buruŋ raven]

crow	burung gagak	[buruŋ gaga ʔ]
jackdaw	burung gagak kecil	[buruŋ gaga ʔ ketʃil]
rook	burung rook	[buruŋ roo ʔ]

duck	bebek	[bebe ʔ]
goose	angsa	[aŋsa]
pheasant	burung kuau	[buruŋ kuau]

eagle	rajawali	[radʒ awali]
hawk	elang	[elaŋ]
falcon	alap-alap	[alap-alap]
vulture	hering	[heriŋ]
condor (Andean ~)	kondor	[kondor]

swan	angsa	[aŋsa]
crane	burung jenjang	[buruŋ dʒ endʒ aŋ]
stork	bangau	[baŋau]

parrot	burung nuri	[buruŋ nuri]
hummingbird	burung kolibri	[buruŋ kolibri]
peacock	burung merak	[buruŋ mera ʔ]

ostrich	burung unta	[buruŋ unta]
heron	kuntul	[kuntul]
flamingo	burung flamingo	[buruŋ flamiŋo]
pelican	pelikan	[pelikan]

| nightingale | burung bulbul | [buruŋ bulbul] |
| swallow | burung walet | [buruŋ walet] |

thrush	burung jalak	[buruŋ dʒ ala ʔ]
song thrush	burung jalak suren	[buruŋ dʒ ala ʔ suren]
blackbird	burung jalak hitam	[buruŋ dʒ ala ʔ hitam]

swift	burung apus-apus	[buruŋ apus-apus]
lark	burung lark	[buruŋ lar ʔ]
quail	burung puyuh	[buruŋ puyuh]

woodpecker	burung pelatuk	[buruŋ pelatu ʔ]
cuckoo	burung kukuk	[buruŋ kuku ʔ]
owl	burung hantu	[buruŋ hantu]
eagle owl	burung hantu bertanduk	[buruŋ hantu bertandu ʔ]
wood grouse	burung murai kayu	[buruŋ muraj kaju]
black grouse	burung belibis hitam	[buruŋ belibis hitam]
partridge	ayam hutan	[ajam hutan]

starling	burung starling	[buruŋ starliŋ]
canary	burung kenari	[buruŋ kenari]
hazel grouse	ayam hutan hazel	[ajam hutan hazel]

| chaffinch | burung chaffinch | [buruŋ tʃaffintʃ] |
| bullfinch | burung bullfinch | [buruŋ bullfintʃ] |

seagull	burung camar	[buruŋ tʃamar]
albatross	albatros	[albatros]
penguin	penguin	[peŋuin]

91. Fish. Marine animals

bream	**ikan bream**	[ikan bream]
carp	**ikan karper**	[ikan karper]
perch	**ikan tilapia**	[ikan tilapia]
catfish	**lais junggang**	[lajs dʒiuŋgaŋ]
pike	**ikan pike**	[ikan paik]
salmon	**salmon**	[salmon]
sturgeon	**ikan sturgeon**	[ikan sturdʒien]
herring	**ikan haring**	[ikan hariŋ]
Atlantic salmon	**ikan salem**	[ikan salem]
mackerel	**ikan kembung**	[ikan kembuŋ]
flatfish	**ikan sebelah**	[ikan sebelah]
zander, pike perch	**ikan seligi tenggeran**	[ikan seligi teŋgeran]
cod	**ikan kod**	[ikan kod]
tuna	**tuna**	[tuna]
trout	**ikan forel**	[ikan forel]
eel	**belut**	[belut]
electric ray	**ikan pari listrik**	[ikan pari listri']
moray eel	**belut moray**	[belut morey]
piranha	**ikan piranha**	[ikan piranha]
shark	**ikan hiu**	[ikan hiu]
dolphin	**lumba-lumba**	[lumba-lumba]
whale	**ikan paus**	[ikan paus]
crab	**kepiting**	[kepitiŋ]
jellyfish	**ubur-ubur**	[ubur-ubur]
octopus	**gurita**	[gurita]
starfish	**bintang laut**	[bintaŋ laut]
sea urchin	**landak laut**	[landa' laut]
seahorse	**kuda laut**	[kuda laut]
oyster	**tiram**	[tiram]
prawn	**udang**	[udaŋ]
lobster	**udang karang**	[udaŋ karaŋ]
spiny lobster	**lobster berduri**	[lobster bərduri]

92. Amphibians. Reptiles

snake	**ular**	[ular]
venomous (snake)	**berbisa**	[bərbisa]
viper	**ular viper**	[ular viper]
cobra	**kobra**	[kobra]
python	**ular sanca**	[ular santʃa]
boa	**ular boa**	[ular boa]
grass snake	**ular tanah**	[ular tanah]

| rattle snake | ular derik | [ular deri⁷] |
| anaconda | ular anakonda | [ular anakonda] |

lizard	kadal	[kadal]
iguana	iguana	[iguana]
monitor lizard	biawak	[biawa⁷]
salamander	salamander	[salamander]
chameleon	bunglon	[buŋlon]
scorpion	kalajengking	[kaladʒ'eŋkiŋ]

turtle	kura-kura	[kura-kura]
frog	katak	[kata⁷]
toad	kodok	[kodo⁷]
crocodile	buaya	[buaja]

93. Insects

insect	serangga	[seraŋga]
butterfly	kupu-kupu	[kupu-kupu]
ant	semut	[semut]
fly	lalat	[lalat]
mosquito	nyamuk	[njamu⁷]
beetle	kumbang	[kumbaŋ]

wasp	tawon	[tawon]
bee	lebah	[lebah]
bumblebee	kumbang	[kumbaŋ]
gadfly (botfly)	lalat kerbau	[lalat kerbau]

| spider | laba-laba | [laba-laba] |
| spider's web | sarang laba-laba | [saraŋ laba-laba] |

dragonfly	capung	[tʃapuŋ]
grasshopper	belalang	[belalaŋ]
moth (night butterfly)	ngengat	[ŋeŋat]

cockroach	kecoa	[ketʃoa]
tick	kutu	[kutu]
flea	kutu loncat	[kutu lontʃat]
midge	agas	[agas]

locust	belalang	[belalaŋ]
snail	siput	[siput]
cricket	jangkrik	[dʒ'aŋkri⁷]
firefly	kunang-kunang	[kunaŋ-kunaŋ]
ladybird	kumbang koksi	[kumbaŋ koksi]
cockchafer	kumbang Cockchafer	[kumbaŋ kokʃafer]

leech	lintah	[lintah]
caterpillar	ulat	[ulat]
earthworm	cacing	[tʃatʃiŋ]
larva	larva	[larva]

FLORA

94. Trees

tree	**pohon**	[pohon]
deciduous (adj)	**daun luruh**	[daun luruh]
coniferous (adj)	**pohon jarum**	[pohon dʒｌarum]
evergreen (adj)	**selalu hijau**	[selalu hidʒｌau]
apple tree	**pohon apel**	[pohon apel]
pear tree	**pohon pir**	[pohon pir]
sweet cherry tree	**pohon ceri manis**	[pohon tʃeri manis]
sour cherry tree	**pohon ceri asam**	[pohon tʃeri asam]
plum tree	**pohon plum**	[pohon plum]
birch	**pohon berk**	[pohon berʔ]
oak	**pohon eik**	[pohon eiʔ]
linden tree	**pohon linden**	[pohon linden]
aspen	**pohon aspen**	[pohon aspen]
maple	**pohon mapel**	[pohon mapel]
spruce	**pohon den**	[pohon den]
pine	**pohon pinus**	[pohon pinus]
larch	**pohon larch**	[pohon lartʃ]
fir tree	**pohon fir**	[pohon fir]
cedar	**pohon aras**	[pohon aras]
poplar	**pohon poplar**	[pohon poplar]
rowan	**pohon rowan**	[pohon rowan]
willow	**pohon dedalu**	[pohon dedalu]
alder	**pohon alder**	[pohon alder]
beech	**pohon nothofagus**	[pohon notofagus]
elm	**pohon elm**	[pohon elm]
ash (tree)	**pohon abu**	[pohon abu]
chestnut	**kastanye**	[kastanje]
magnolia	**magnolia**	[magnolia]
palm tree	**palem**	[palem]
cypress	**pokok cipres**	[pokoʔ sipres]
mangrove	**bakau**	[bakau]
baobab	**baobab**	[baobab]
eucalyptus	**kayu putih**	[kaju putih]
sequoia	**sequoia**	[sekuoia]

95. Shrubs

bush	**rumpun**	[rumpun]
shrub	**semak**	[semaʔ]

| grapevine | pohon anggur | [pohon aŋgur] |
| vineyard | kebun anggur | [kebun aŋgur] |

raspberry bush	pohon frambus	[pohon frambus]
blackcurrant bush	pohon blackcurrant	[pohon ble'karen]
redcurrant bush	pohon redcurrant	[pohon redkaren]
gooseberry bush	pohon arbei hijau	[pohon arbei hiʤⁱau]

acacia	pohon akasia	[pohon akasia]
barberry	pohon barberis	[pohon barberis]
jasmine	melati	[melati]

juniper	pohon juniper	[pohon ʤⁱuniper]
rosebush	pohon mawar	[pohon mawar]
dog rose	pohon mawar liar	[pohon mawar liar]

96. Fruits. Berries

| fruit | buah | [buah] |
| fruits | buah-buahan | [buah-buahan] |

apple	apel	[apel]
pear	pir	[pir]
plum	plum	[plum]

strawberry (garden ~)	stroberi	[stroberi]
sour cherry	buah ceri asam	[buah ʧeri asam]
sweet cherry	buah ceri manis	[buah ʧeri manis]
grape	buah anggur	[buah aŋgur]

raspberry	buah frambus	[buah frambus]
blackcurrant	blackcurrant	[ble'karen]
redcurrant	redcurrant	[redkaren]
gooseberry	buah arbei hijau	[buah arbei hiʤⁱau]
cranberry	buah kranberi	[buah kranberi]

orange	jeruk manis	[ʤⁱeru' manis]
tangerine	jeruk mandarin	[ʤⁱeru' mandarin]
pineapple	nanas	[nanas]
banana	pisang	[pisaŋ]
date	buah kurma	[buah kurma]

lemon	jeruk sitrun	[ʤⁱeru' sitrun]
apricot	aprikot	[aprikot]
peach	persik	[persi']

| kiwi | kiwi | [kiwi] |
| grapefruit | jeruk Bali | [ʤⁱeru' bali] |

berry	buah beri	[buah beri]
berries	buah-buah beri	[buah-buah beri]
cowberry	buah cowberry	[buah kowberi]
wild strawberry	stroberi liar	[stroberi liar]
bilberry	buah bilberi	[buah bilberi]

97. Flowers. Plants

flower	**bunga**	[buɲa]
bouquet (of flowers)	**buket**	[buket]
rose (flower)	**mawar**	[mawar]
tulip	**tulip**	[tulip]
carnation	**bunga anyelir**	[buɲa anjelir]
gladiolus	**bunga gladiol**	[buɲa gladiol]
cornflower	**cornflower**	[kornflawa]
harebell	**bunga lonceng biru**	[buɲa lontʃeŋ biru]
dandelion	**dandelion**	[dandelion]
camomile	**bunga margrit**	[buɲa margrit]
aloe	**lidah buaya**	[lidah buaja]
cactus	**kaktus**	[kaktus]
rubber plant, ficus	**pohon ara**	[pohon ara]
lily	**bunga lili**	[buɲa lili]
geranium	**geranium**	[geranium]
hyacinth	**bunga bakung lembayung**	[buɲa bakuŋ lembajuŋ]
mimosa	**putri malu**	[putri malu]
narcissus	**bunga narsis**	[buɲa narsis]
nasturtium	**bunga nasturtium**	[buɲa nasturtium]
orchid	**anggrek**	[aŋgreʔ]
peony	**bunga peoni**	[buɲa peoni]
violet	**bunga violet**	[buɲa violet]
pansy	**bunga pansy**	[buɲa pansi]
forget-me-not	**bunga jangan-lupakan-daku**	[buɲa dʒʲaŋan-lupakan-daku]
daisy	**bunga desi**	[buɲa desi]
poppy	**bunga madat**	[buɲa madat]
hemp	**rami**	[rami]
mint	**mint**	[min]
lily of the valley	**lili lembah**	[lili lembah]
snowdrop	**bunga tetesan salju**	[buɲa tetesan saldʒʲu]
nettle	**jelatang**	[dʒʲelataŋ]
sorrel	**daun sorrel**	[daun sorrel]
water lily	**lili air**	[lili air]
fern	**pakis**	[pakis]
lichen	**lichen**	[litʃen]
conservatory (greenhouse)	**rumah kaca**	[rumah katʃa]
lawn	**halaman berumput**	[halaman bərumput]
flowerbed	**bedeng bunga**	[bedeŋ buɲa]
plant	**tumbuhan**	[tumbuhan]
grass	**rumput**	[rumput]

blade of grass	**sehelai rumput**	[sehelaj rumput]
leaf	**daun**	[daun]
petal	**kelopak**	[kelopa']
stem	**batang**	[bataŋ]
tuber	**ubi**	[ubi]
young plant (shoot)	**tunas**	[tunas]
thorn	**duri**	[duri]
to blossom (vi)	**berbunga**	[bərbuŋa]
to fade, to wither	**layu**	[laju]
smell (odour)	**bau**	[bau]
to cut (flowers)	**memotong**	[memotoŋ]
to pick (a flower)	**memetik**	[memeti']

98. Cereals, grains

grain	**biji-bijian**	[bidʒi-bidʒian]
cereal crops	**padi-padian**	[padi-padian]
ear (of barley, etc.)	**bulir**	[bulir]
wheat	**gandum**	[gandum]
rye	**gandum hitam**	[gandum hitam]
oats	**oat**	[oat]
millet	**jawawut**	[dʒˈawawut]
barley	**jelai**	[dʒˈelaj]
maize	**jagung**	[dʒˈaguŋ]
rice	**beras**	[beras]
buckwheat	**buckwheat**	[bakvit]
pea plant	**kacang polong**	[katʃaŋ poloŋ]
kidney bean	**kacang buncis**	[katʃaŋ buntʃis]
soya	**kacang kedelai**	[katʃaŋ kedelaj]
lentil	**kacang lentil**	[katʃaŋ lentil]
beans (pulse crops)	**kacang-kacangan**	[katʃaŋ-katʃaŋan]

COUNTRIES OF THE WORLD

99. Countries. Part 1

Afghanistan	**Afghanistan**	[afganistan]
Albania	**Albania**	[albania]
Argentina	**Argentina**	[argentina]
Armenia	**Armenia**	[armenia]
Australia	**Australia**	[australia]
Austria	**Austria**	[austria]
Azerbaijan	**Azerbaijan**	[azerbajdʒian]
The Bahamas	**Kepulauan Bahama**	[kepulauan bahama]
Bangladesh	**Bangladesh**	[baŋladeʃ]
Belarus	**Belarusia**	[belarusia]
Belgium	**Belgia**	[belgia]
Bolivia	**Bolivia**	[bolivia]
Bosnia and Herzegovina	**Bosnia-Hercegovina**	[bosnia-hersegovina]
Brazil	**Brasil**	[brasil]
Bulgaria	**Bulgaria**	[bulgaria]
Cambodia	**Kamboja**	[kambodʒia]
Canada	**Kanada**	[kanada]
Chile	**Chili**	[tʃili]
China	**Tiongkok**	[tjoŋko']
Colombia	**Kolombia**	[kolombia]
Croatia	**Kroasia**	[kroasia]
Cuba	**Kuba**	[kuba]
Cyprus	**Siprus**	[siprus]
Czech Republic	**Republik Ceko**	[republi' tʃeko]
Denmark	**Denmark**	[denmar']
Dominican Republic	**Republik Dominika**	[republi' dominika]
Ecuador	**Ekuador**	[ekuador]
Egypt	**Mesir**	[mesir]
England	**Inggris**	[iŋgris]
Estonia	**Estonia**	[estonia]
Finland	**Finlandia**	[finlandia]
France	**Prancis**	[prantʃis]
French Polynesia	**Polinesia Prancis**	[polinesia prantʃis]
Georgia	**Georgia**	[dʒordʒia]
Germany	**Jerman**	[dʒierman]
Ghana	**Ghana**	[gana]
Great Britain	**Britania Raya**	[britania raja]
Greece	**Yunani**	[yunani]
Haiti	**Haiti**	[haiti]
Hungary	**Hongaria**	[hoŋaria]

100. Countries. Part 2

Iceland	**Islandia**	[islandia]
India	**India**	[india]
Indonesia	**Indonesia**	[indonesia]
Iran	**Iran**	[iran]
Iraq	**Irak**	[ira']
Ireland	**Irlandia**	[irlandia]
Israel	**Israel**	[israel]
Italy	**Italia**	[italia]
Jamaica	**Jamaika**	[dʒˈamajka]
Japan	**Jepang**	[dʒˈepaŋ]
Jordan	**Yordania**	[yordania]
Kazakhstan	**Kazakistan**	[kazakstan]
Kenya	**Kenya**	[kenia]
Kirghizia	**Kirgizia**	[kirgizia]
Kuwait	**Kuwait**	[kuweyt]
Laos	**Laos**	[laos]
Latvia	**Latvia**	[latvia]
Lebanon	**Lebanon**	[lebanon]
Libya	**Libia**	[libia]
Liechtenstein	**Liechtenstein**	[lajhtensteyn]
Lithuania	**Lituania**	[lituania]
Luxembourg	**Luksemburg**	[luksemburg]
North Macedonia	**Makedonia**	[makedonia]
Madagascar	**Madagaskar**	[madagaskar]
Malaysia	**Malaysia**	[malajsia]
Malta	**Malta**	[malta]
Mexico	**Meksiko**	[meksiko]
Moldova, Moldavia	**Moldova**	[moldova]
Monaco	**Monako**	[monako]
Mongolia	**Mongolia**	[moŋolia]
Montenegro	**Montenegro**	[montenegro]
Morocco	**Maroko**	[maroko]
Myanmar	**Myanmar**	[myanmar]
Namibia	**Namibia**	[namibia]
Nepal	**Nepal**	[nepal]
Netherlands	**Belanda**	[belanda]
New Zealand	**Selandia Baru**	[selandia baru]
North Korea	**Korea Utara**	[korea utara]
Norway	**Norwegia**	[norwegia]

101. Countries. Part 3

Pakistan	**Pakistan**	[pakistan]
Palestine	**Palestina**	[palestina]
Panama	**Panama**	[panama]
Paraguay	**Paraguay**	[paraguaj]

Peru	**Peru**	[peru]
Poland	**Polandia**	[polandia]
Portugal	**Portugal**	[portugal]
Romania	**Romania**	[romania]
Russia	**Rusia**	[rusia]
Saudi Arabia	**Arab Saudi**	[arab saudi]
Scotland	**Skotlandia**	[skotlandia]
Senegal	**Senegal**	[senegal]
Serbia	**Serbia**	[serbia]
Slovakia	**Slowakia**	[slowakia]
Slovenia	**Slovenia**	[slovenia]
South Africa	**Afrika Selatan**	[afrika selatan]
South Korea	**Korea Selatan**	[korea selatan]
Spain	**Spanyol**	[spanjol]
Suriname	**Suriname**	[suriname]
Sweden	**Swedia**	[swedia]
Switzerland	**Swiss**	[swiss]
Syria	**Suriah**	[suriah]
Taiwan	**Taiwan**	[tajwan]
Tajikistan	**Tajikistan**	[tadʒikistan]
Tanzania	**Tanzania**	[tanzania]
Tasmania	**Tasmania**	[tasmania]
Thailand	**Thailand**	[tajland]
Tunisia	**Tunisia**	[tunisia]
Turkey	**Turki**	[turki]
Turkmenistan	**Turkmenistan**	[turkmenistan]
Ukraine	**Ukraina**	[ukrajna]
United Arab Emirates	**Uni Emirat Arab**	[uni emirat arab]
United States of America	**Amerika Serikat**	[amerika serikat]
Uruguay	**Uruguay**	[uruguaj]
Uzbekistan	**Uzbekistan**	[uzbekistan]
Vatican City	**Vatikan**	[vatikan]
Venezuela	**Venezuela**	[venezuela]
Vietnam	**Vietnam**	[vjetnam]
Zanzibar	**Zanzibar**	[zanzibar]

www.ingramcontent.com/pod-product-compliance
Lightning Source LLC
Chambersburg PA
CBHW070822050426
42452CB00011B/2153